I0488985

Step-By-Step Guide To Drawing Your Cat

Collection of Cats Drawing Guide

Cats

By : Gala Publication

Published By :

Gala Publication

© Copyright 2015 – Gala Publication

ISBN-13: **978-1522708674**
ISBN-10: **1522708677**

Table of Contents

CARTOON
CAT

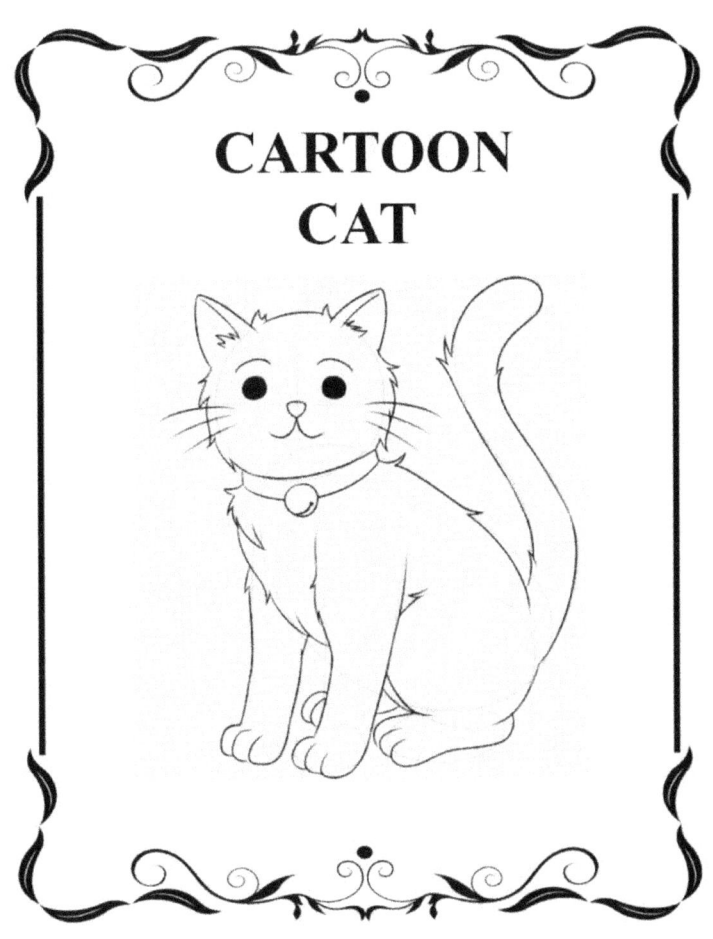

STEP 1

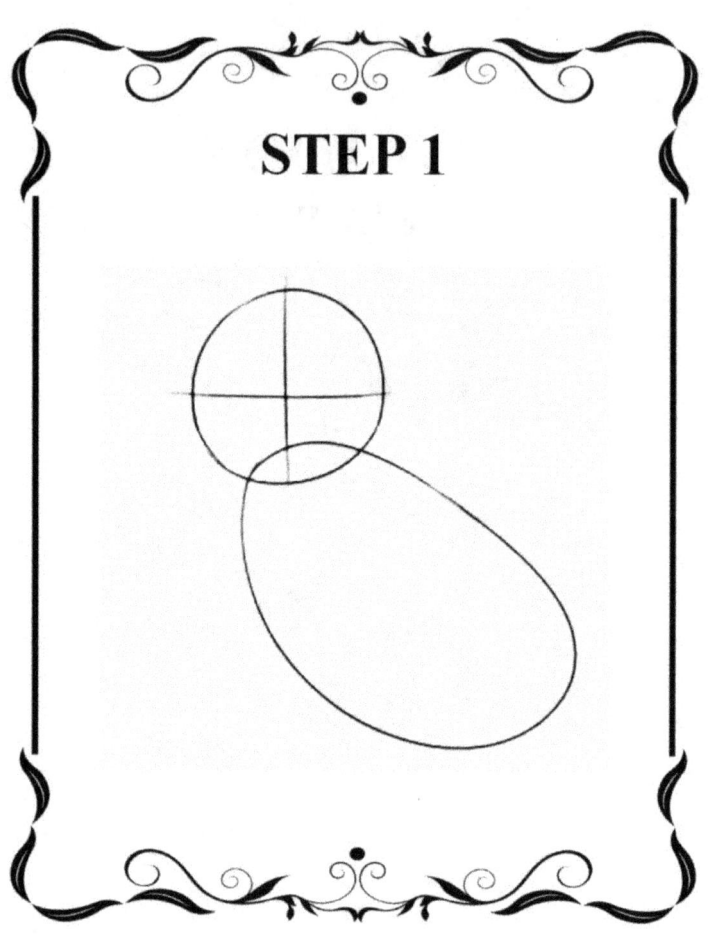

STEP 2

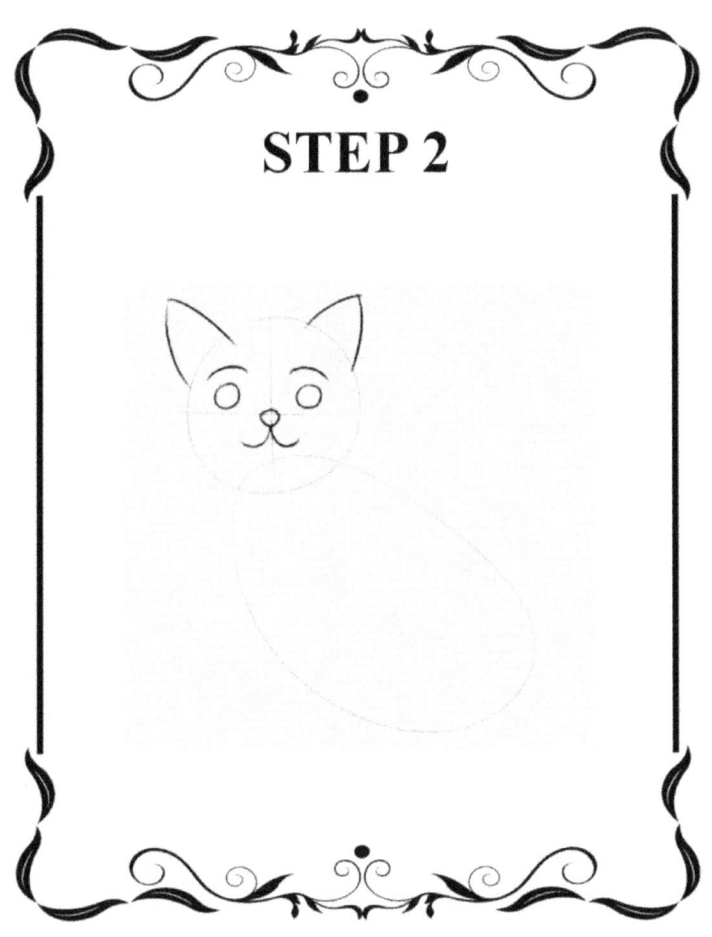

STEP 3

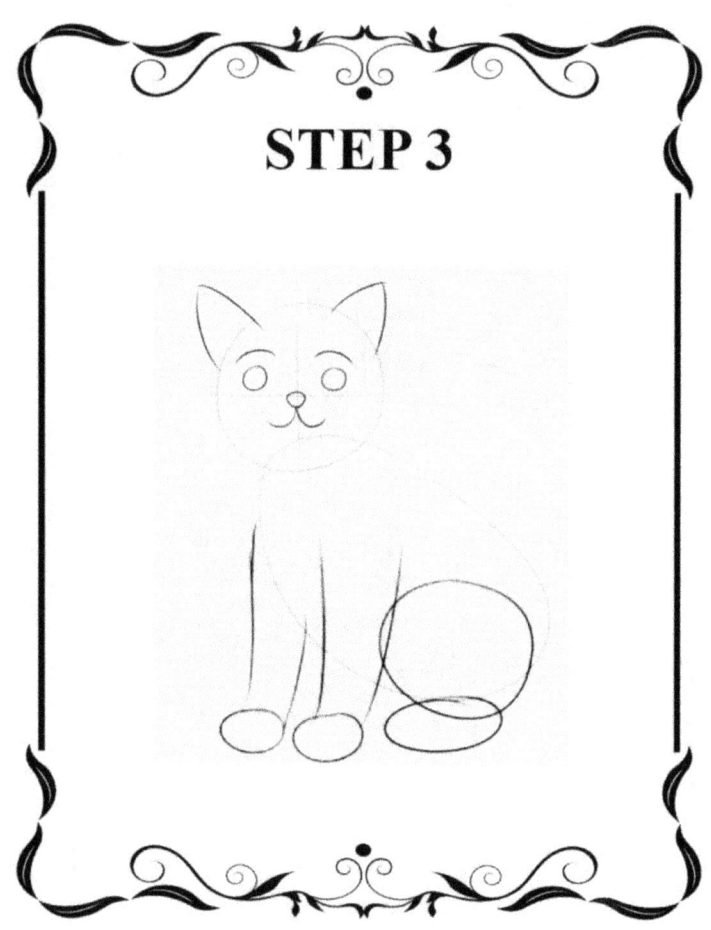

STEP 4

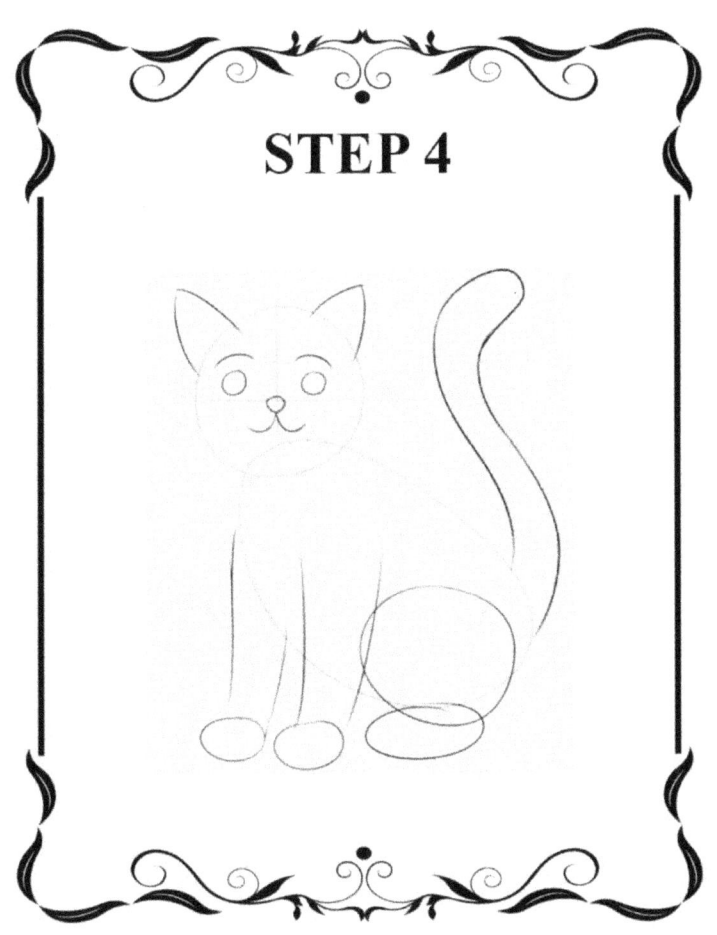

STEP 5

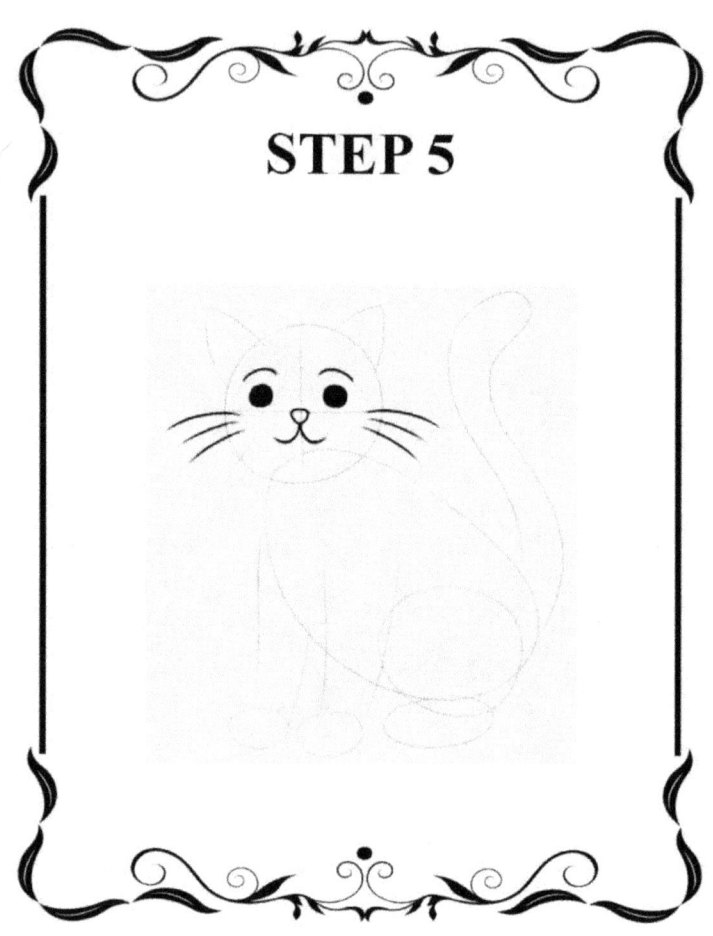

STEP 6

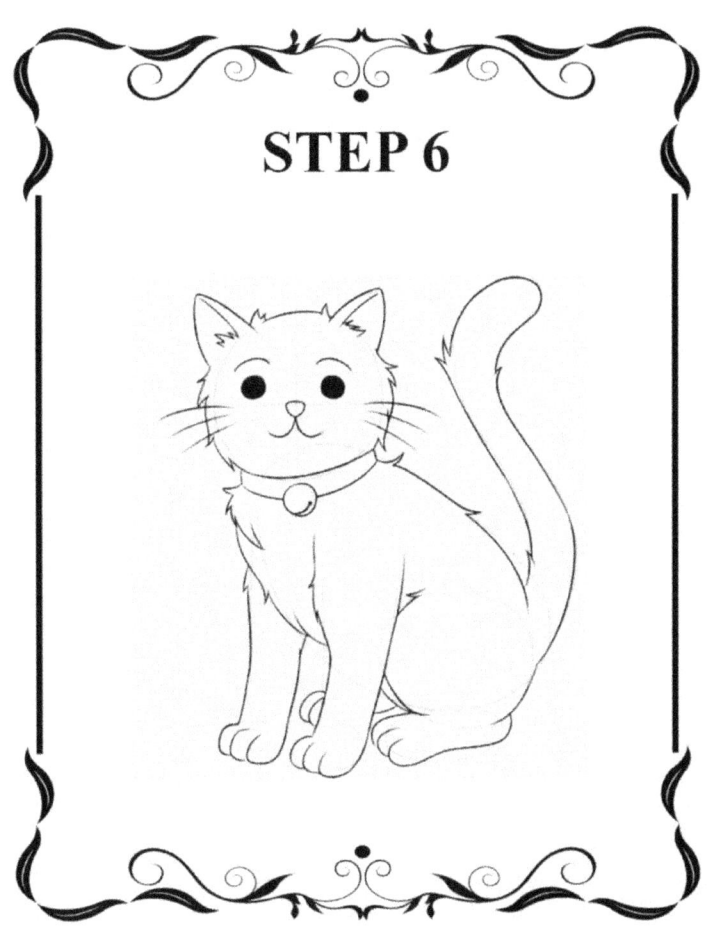

REALISTIC
CAT

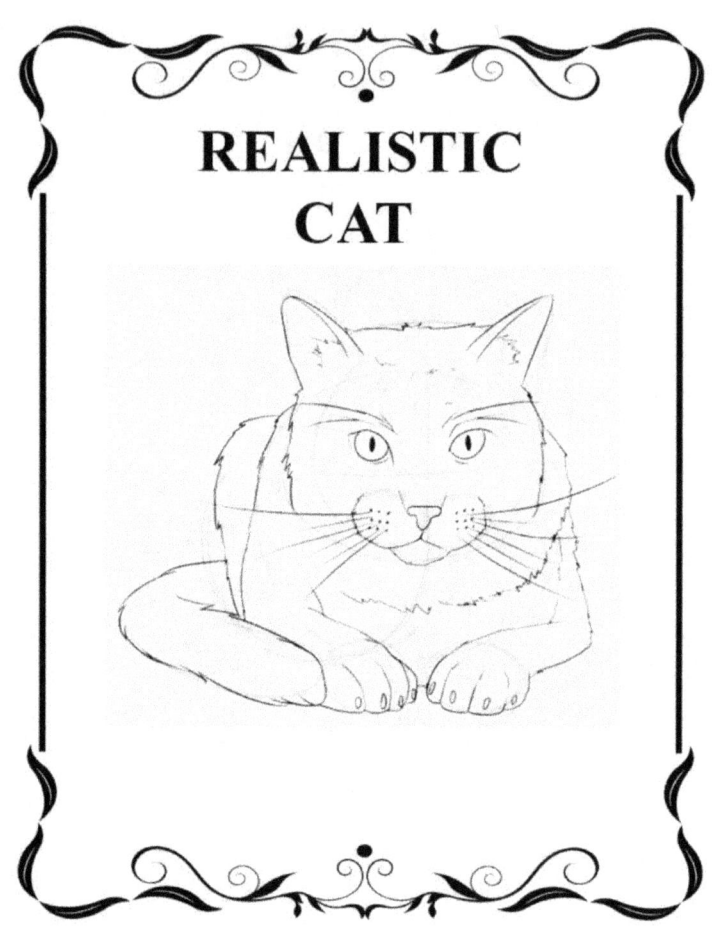

STEP 1

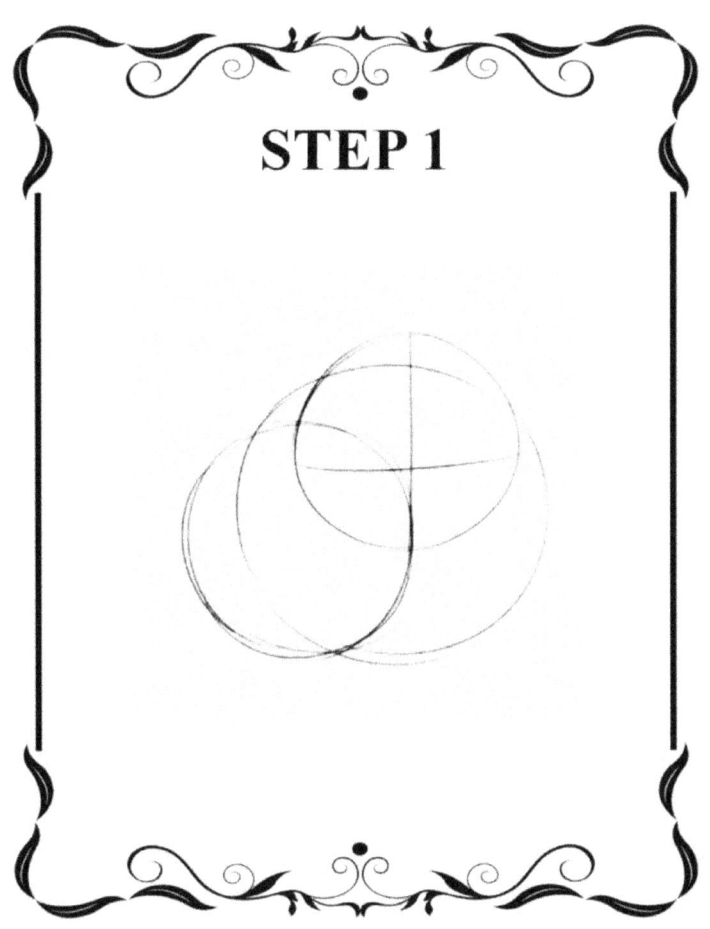

STEP 2

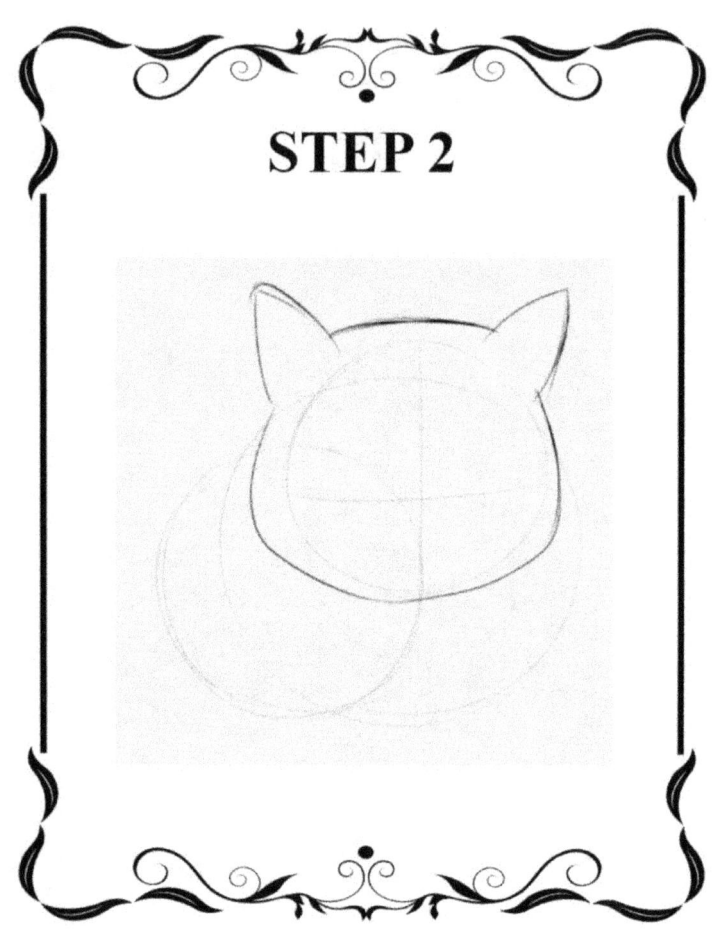

STEP 3

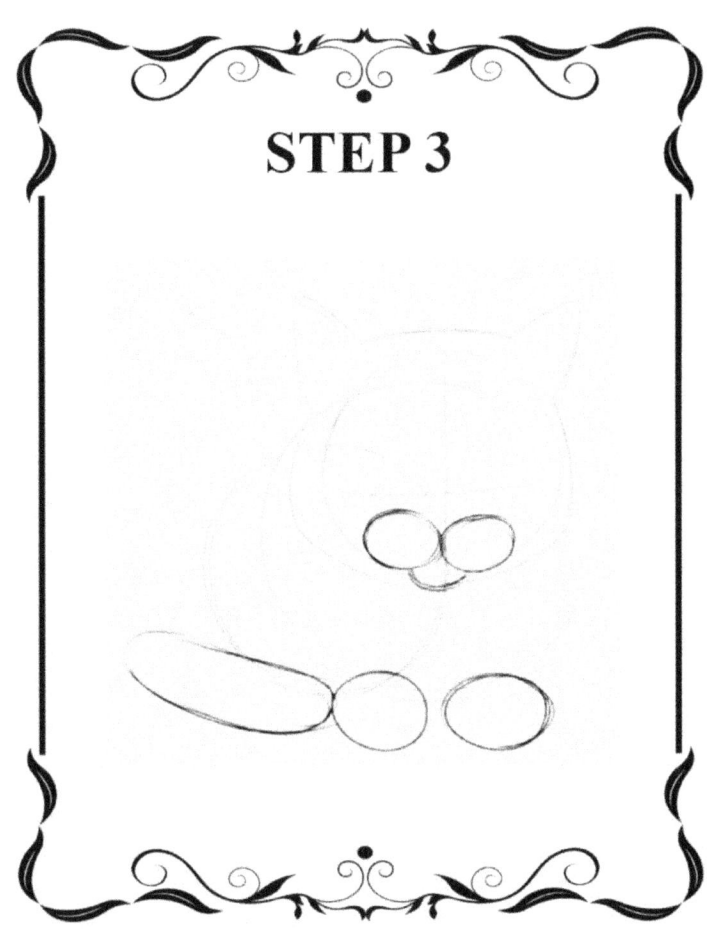

STEP 4

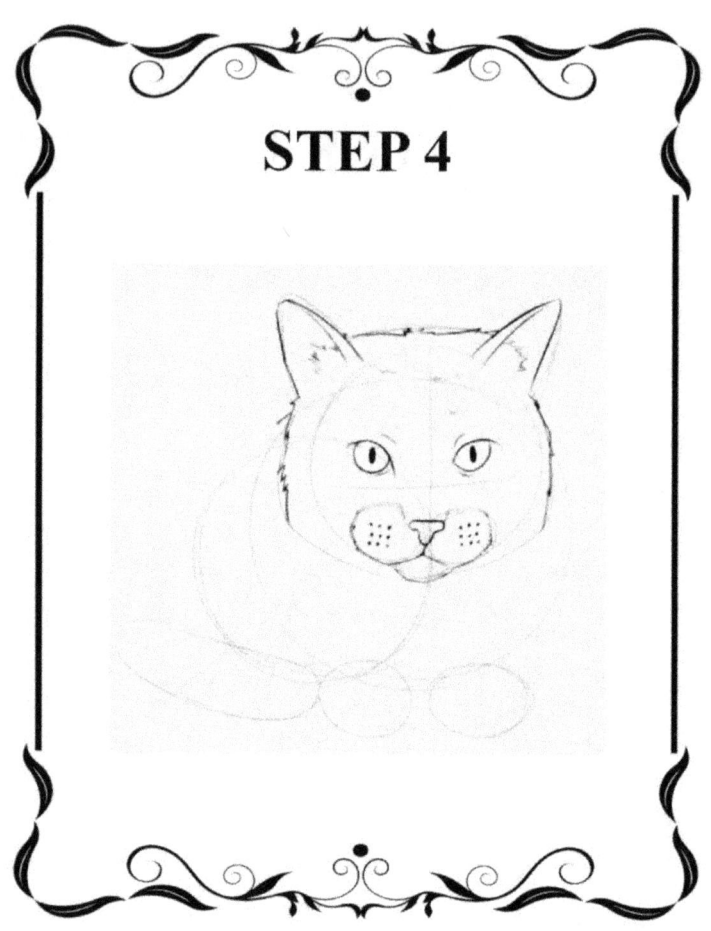

STEP 5

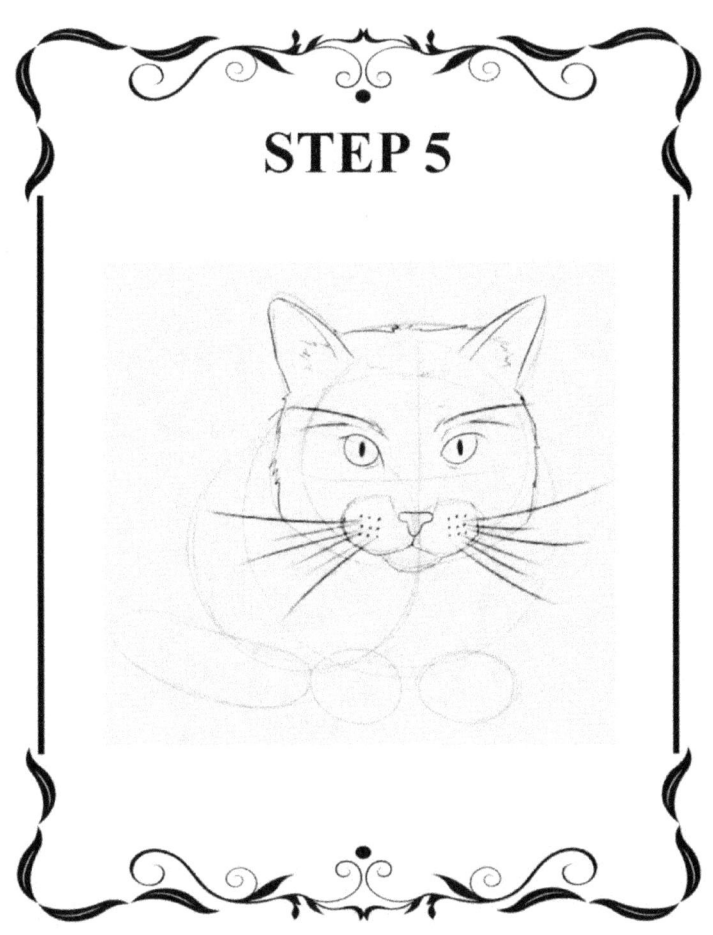

STEP 6

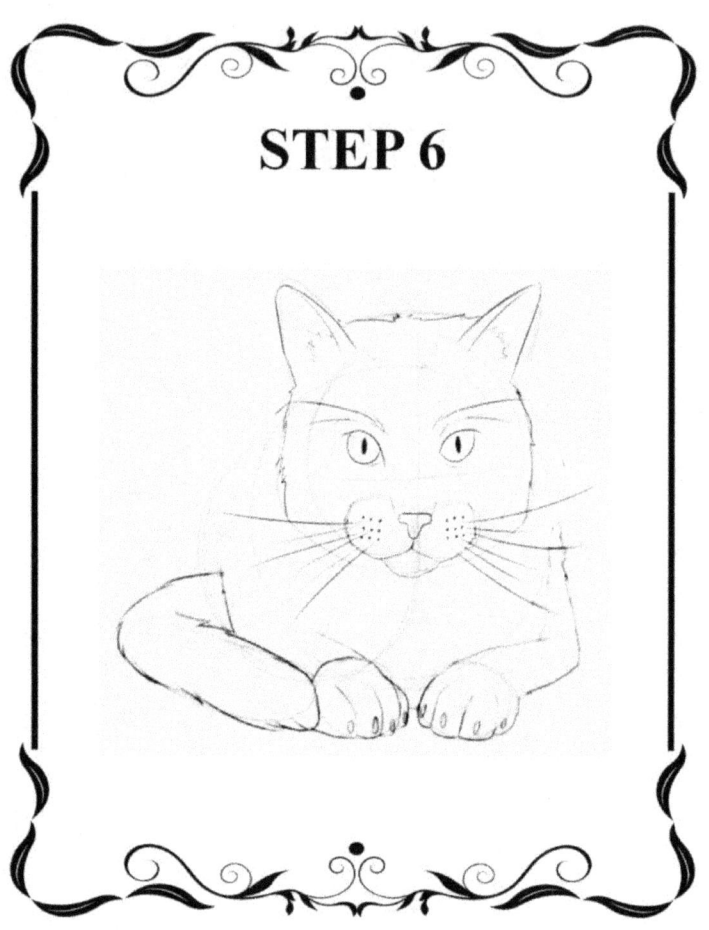

STEP 7

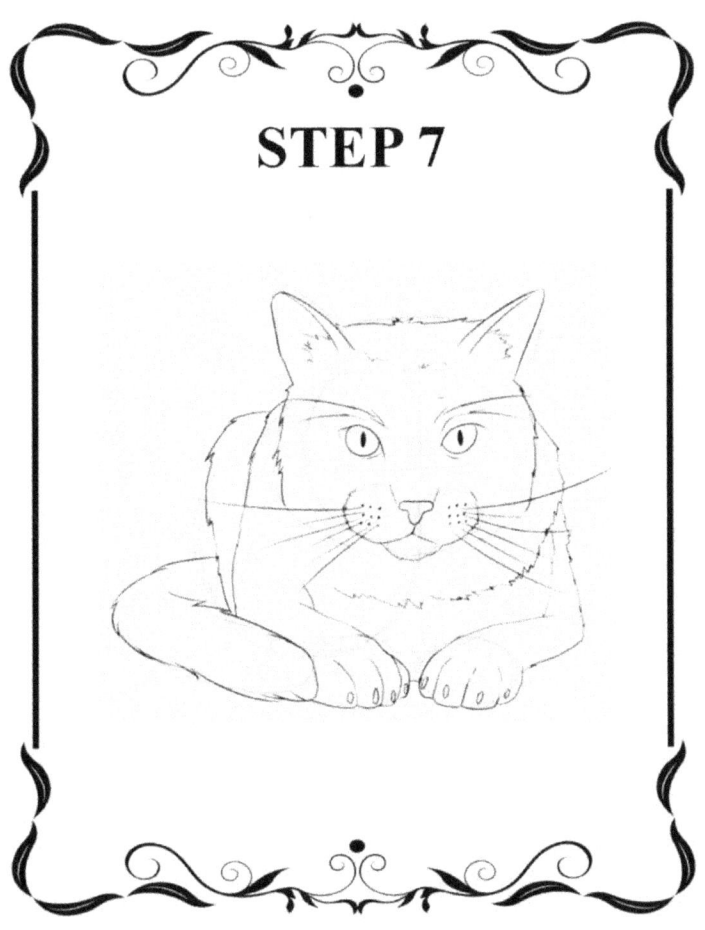

RESTING
CAT

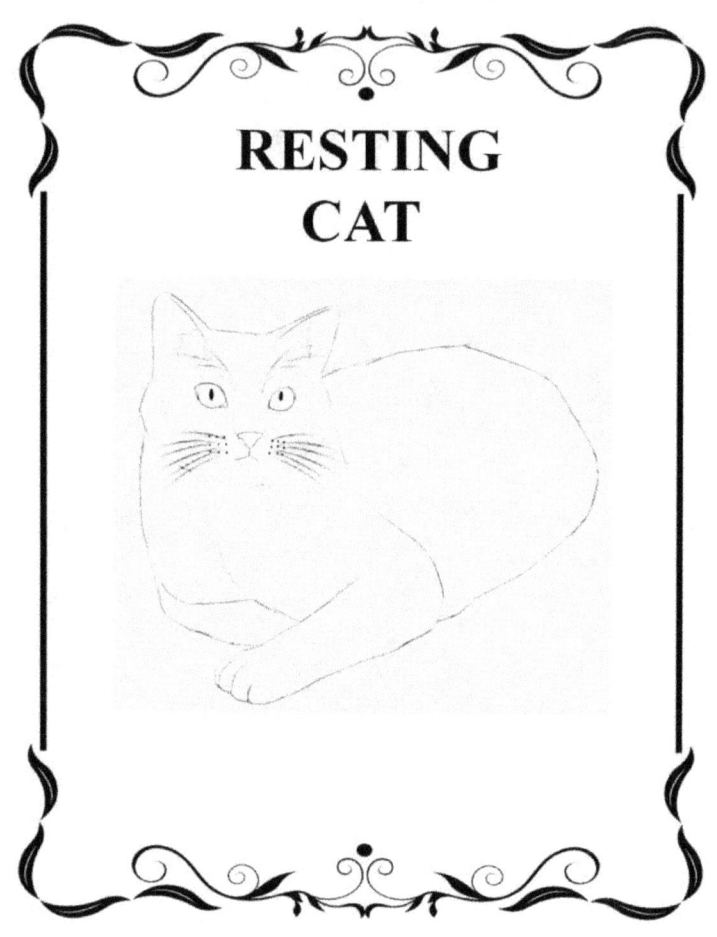

STEP 1

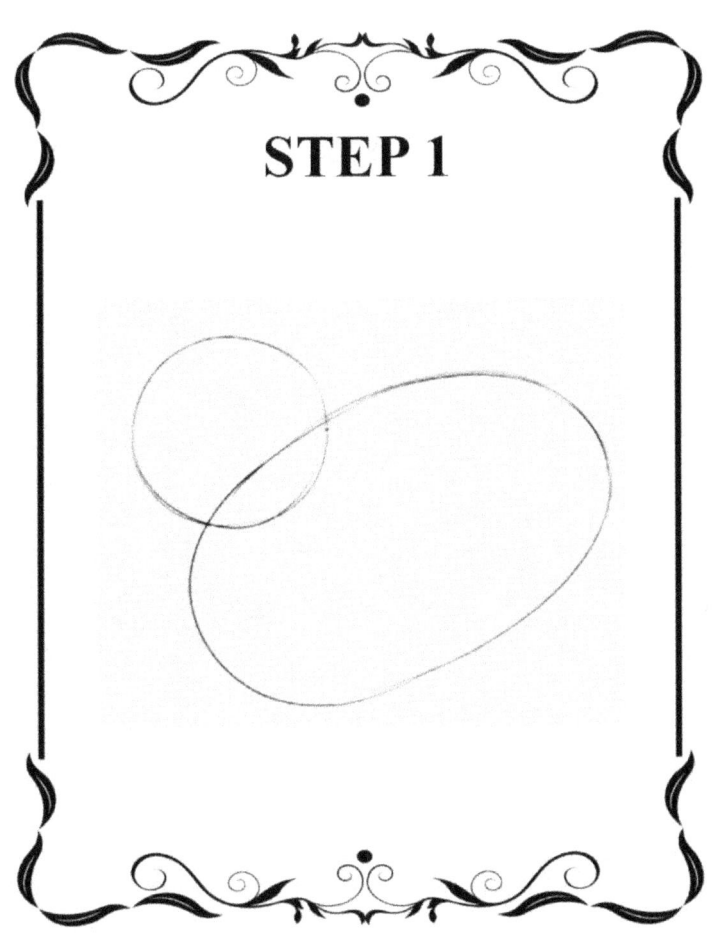

STEP 2

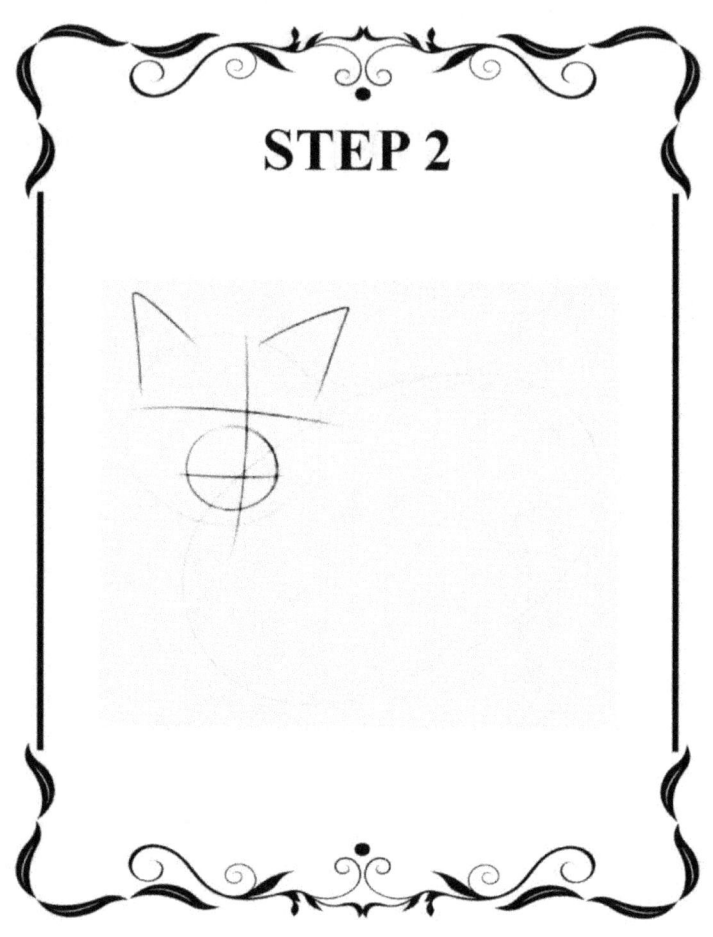

STEP 3

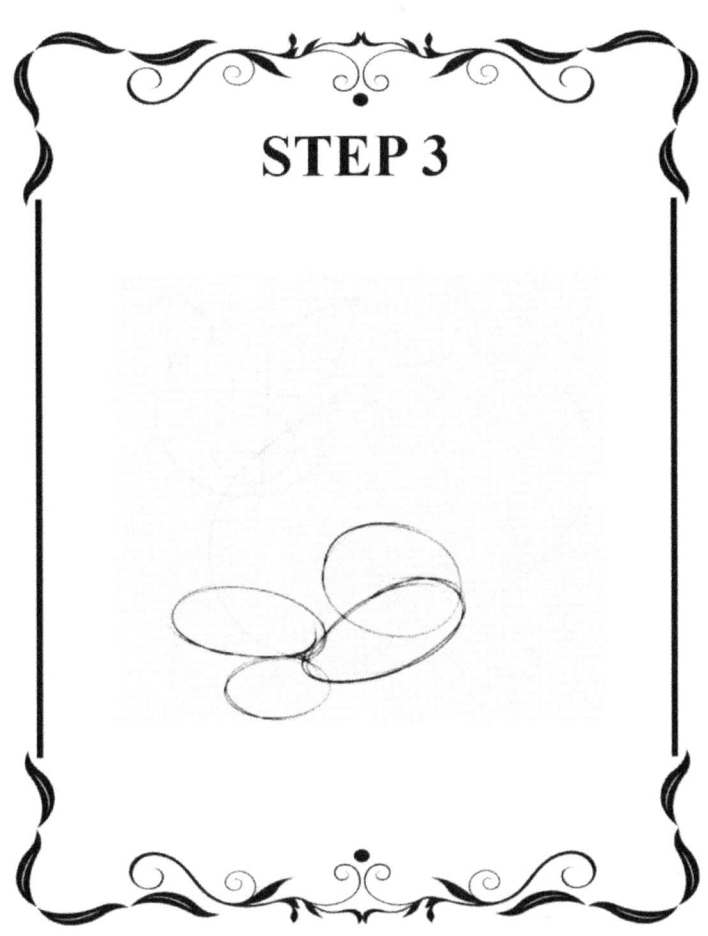

STEP 4

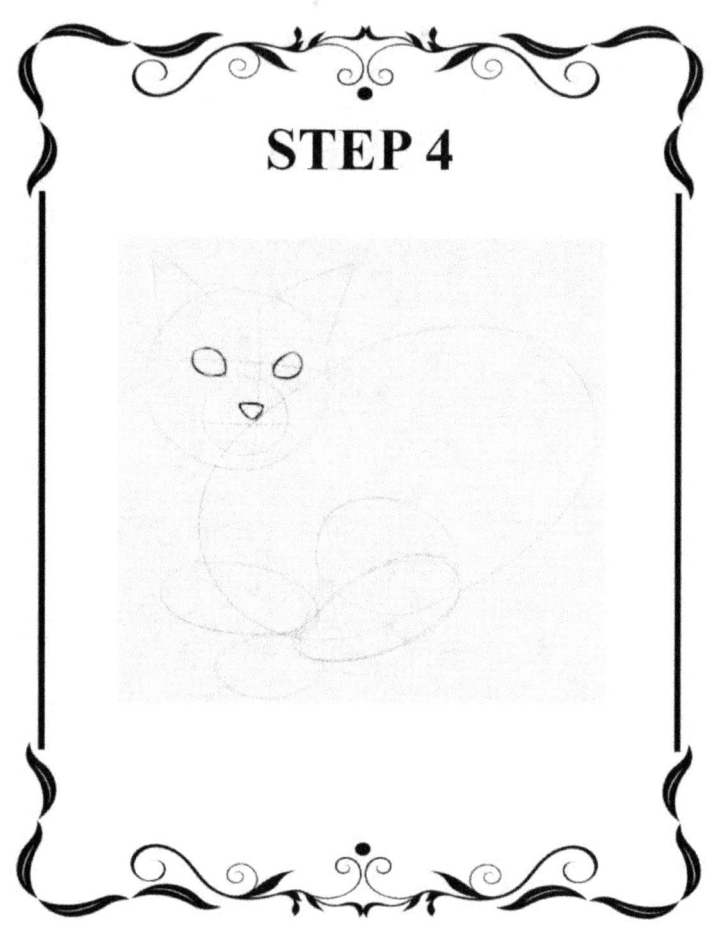

STEP 5

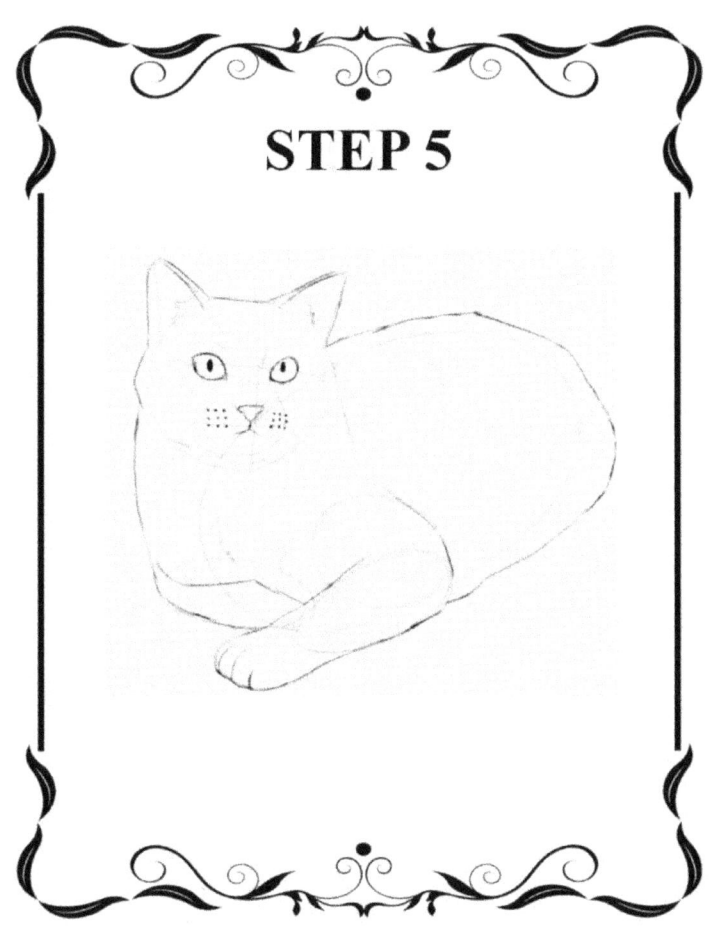

STEP 6

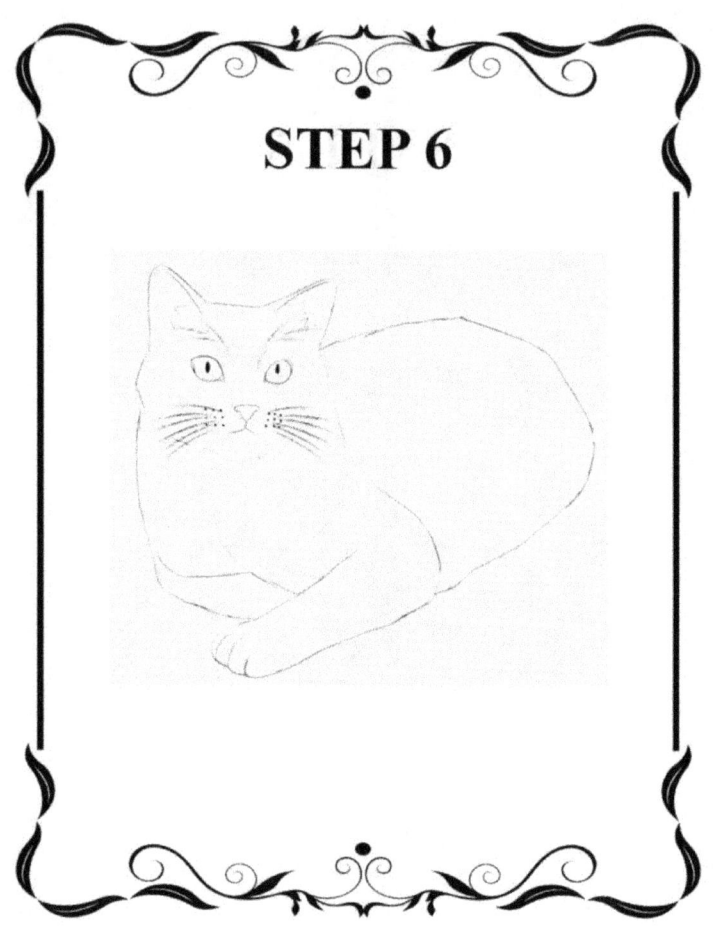

SIAMESE
CAT

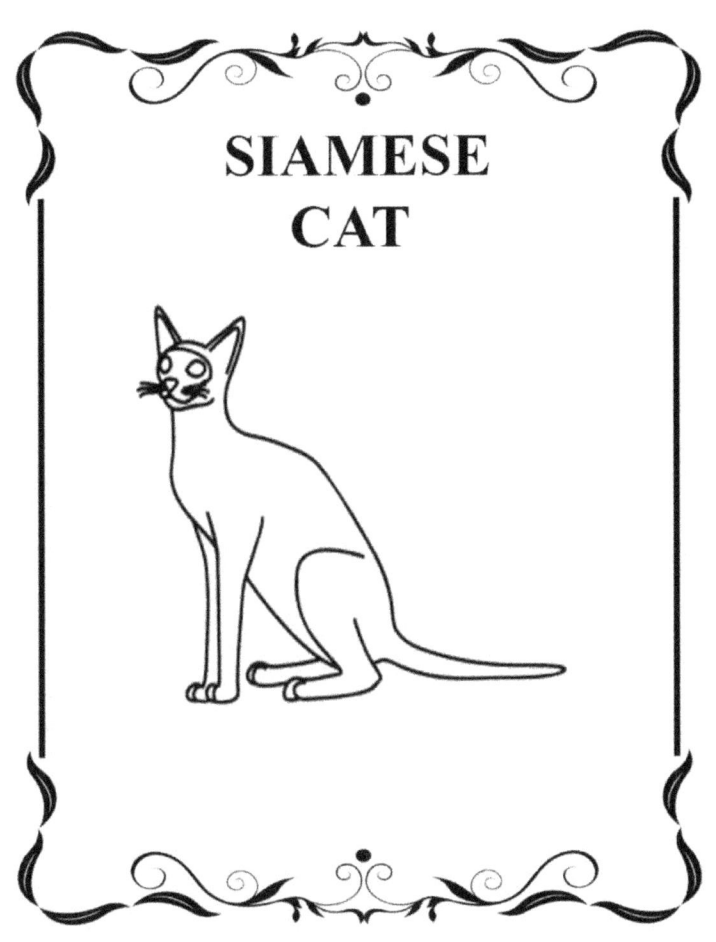

STEP 1

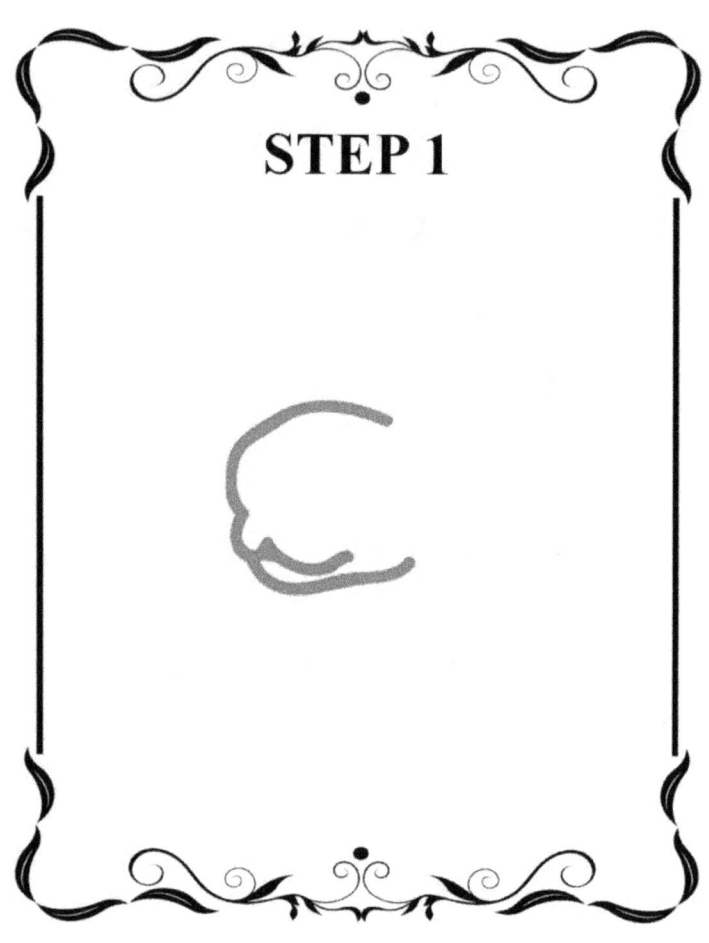

STEP 2

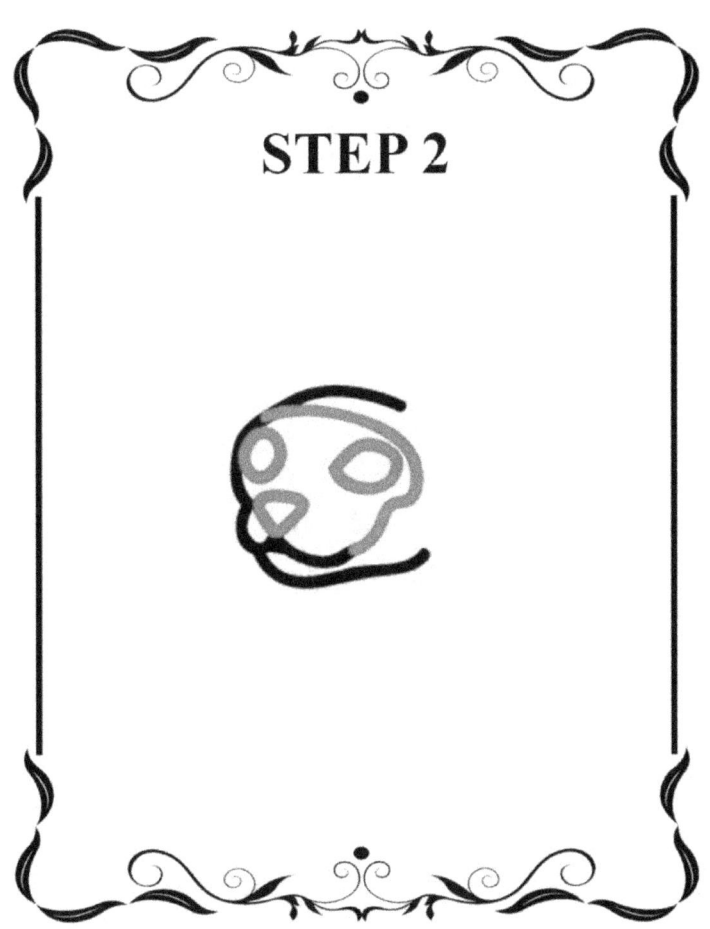

STEP 3

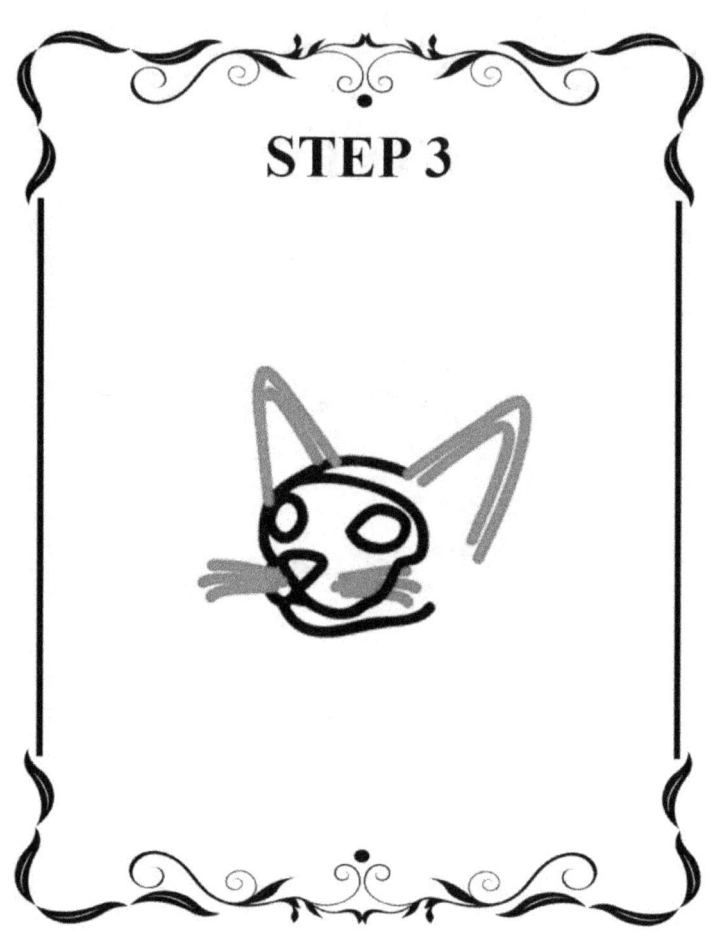

STEP 4

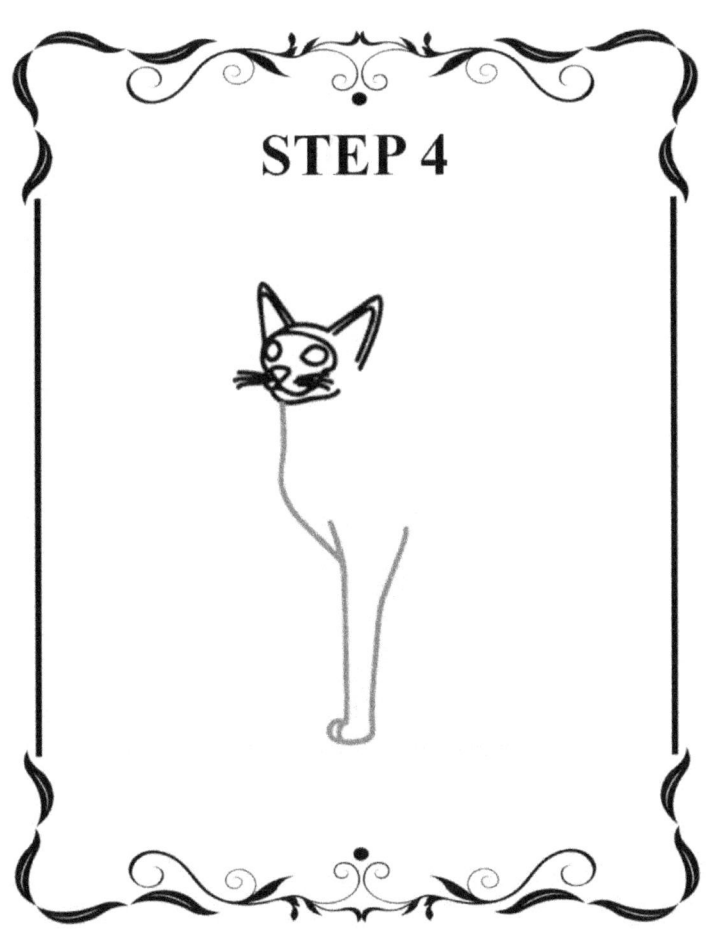

STEP 5

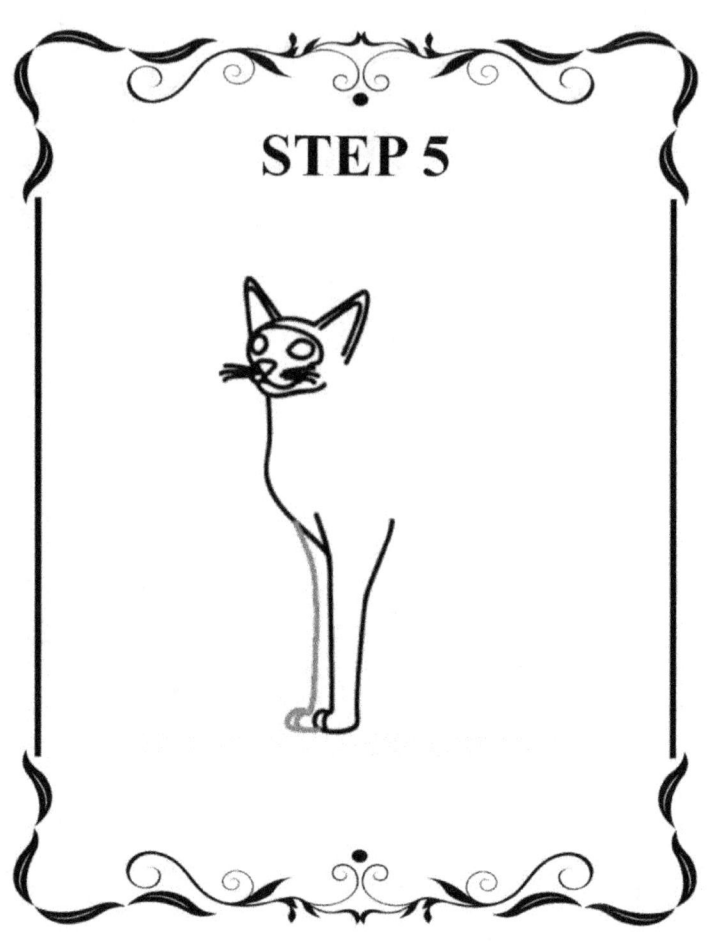

STEP 6

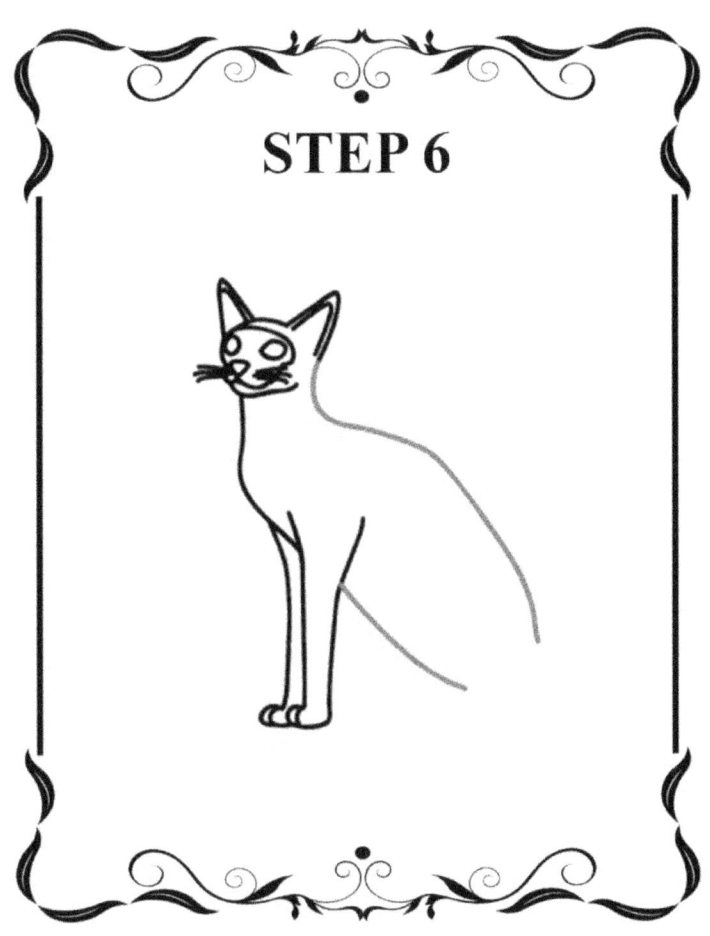

STEP 7

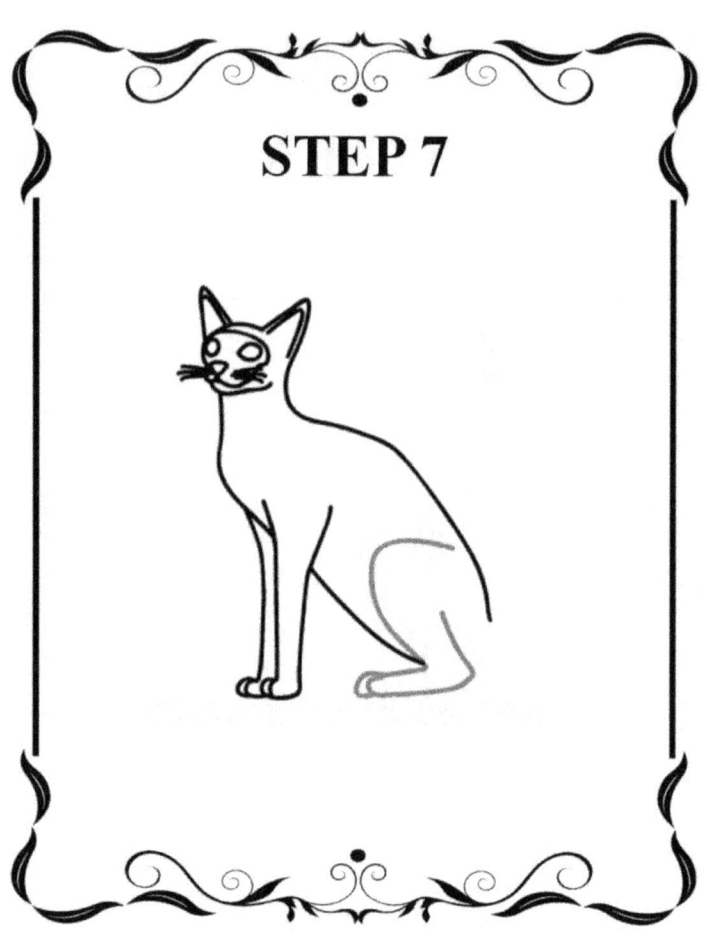

STEP 8

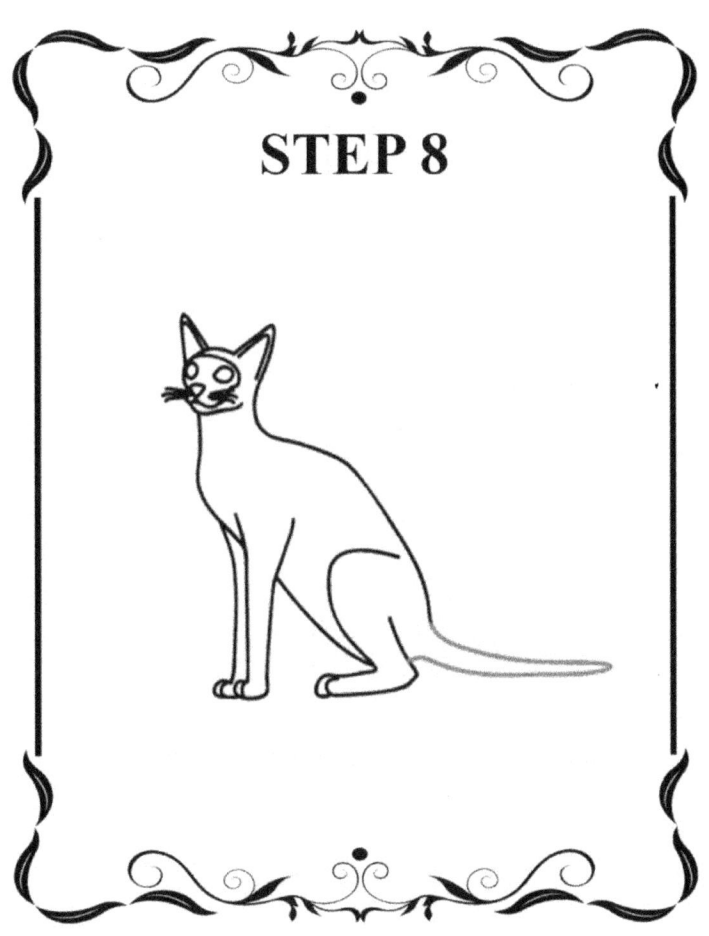

STEP 9

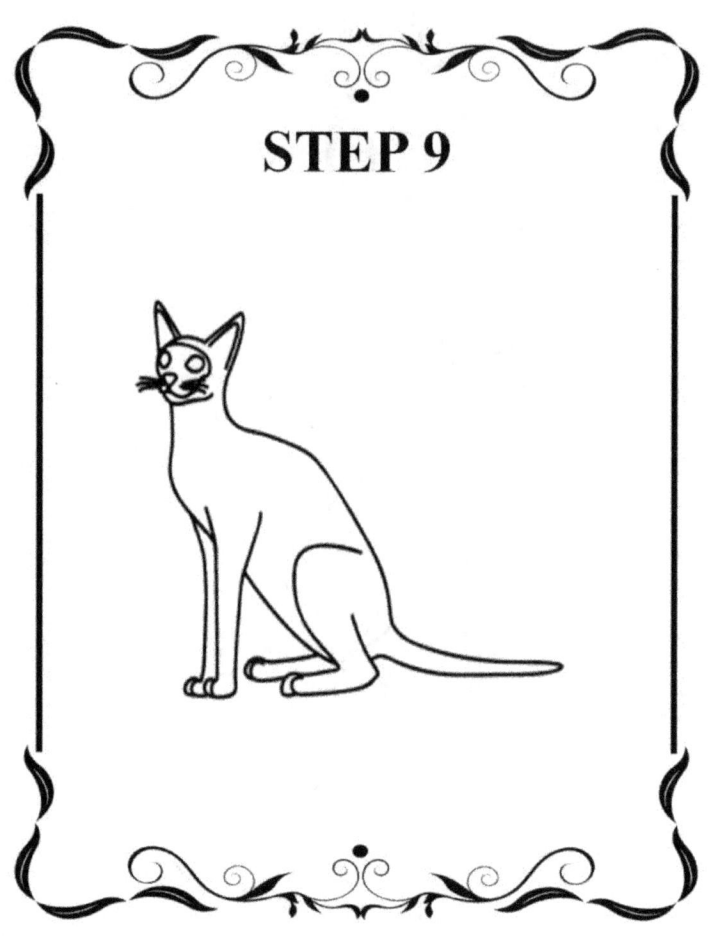

SIMPLE
CAT

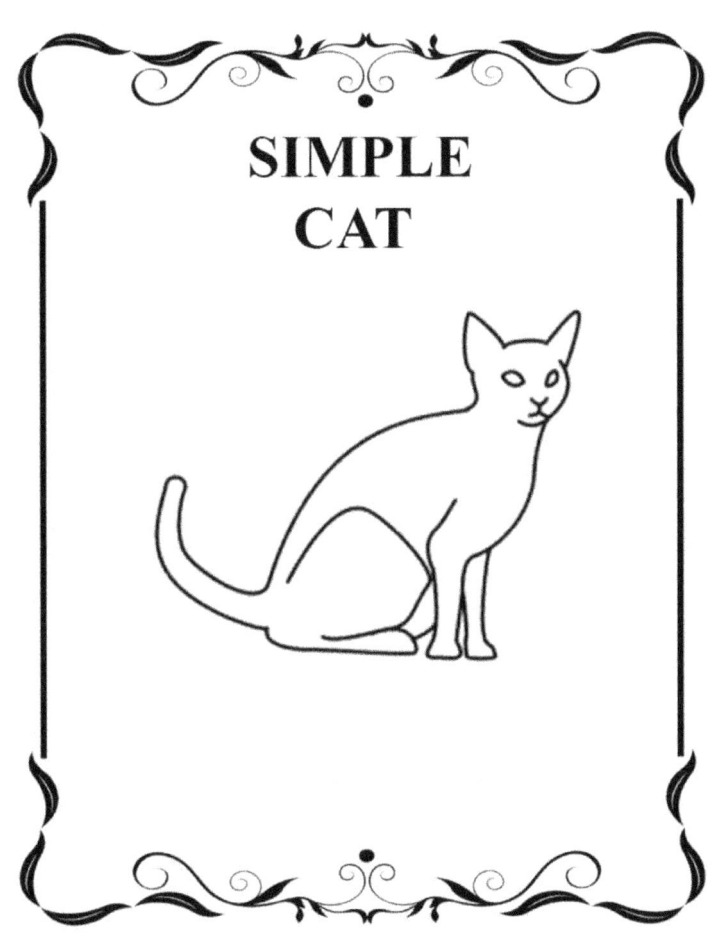

STEP 1

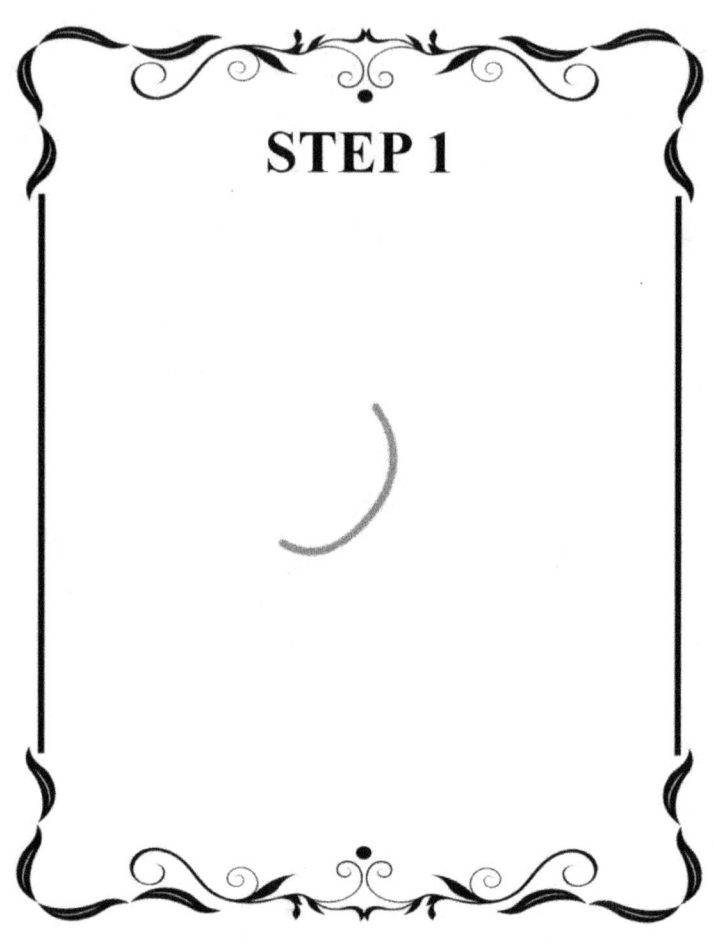

STEP 2

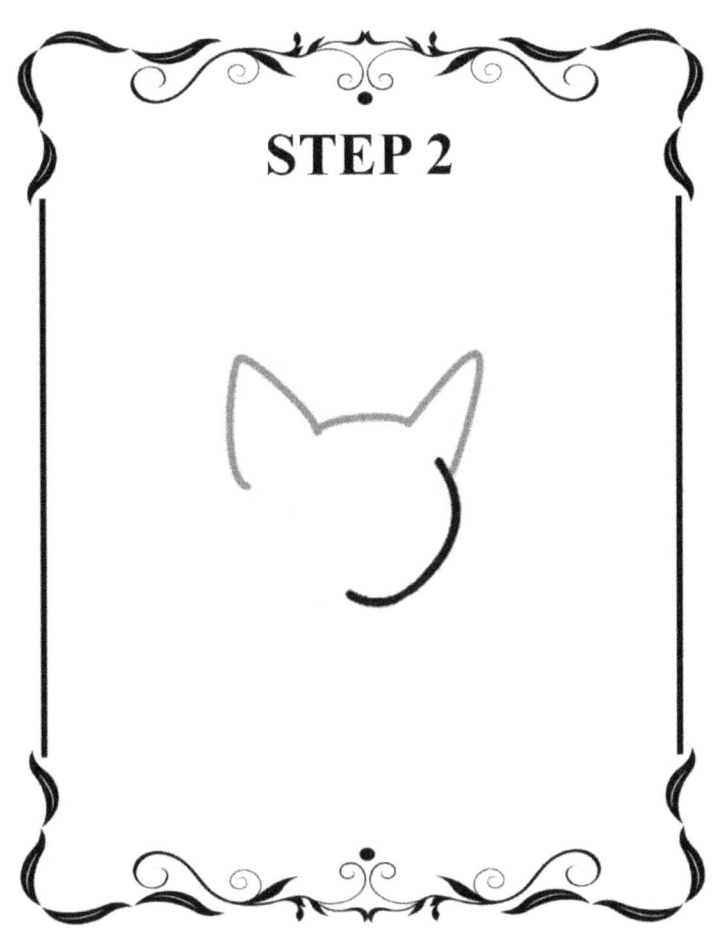

STEP 3

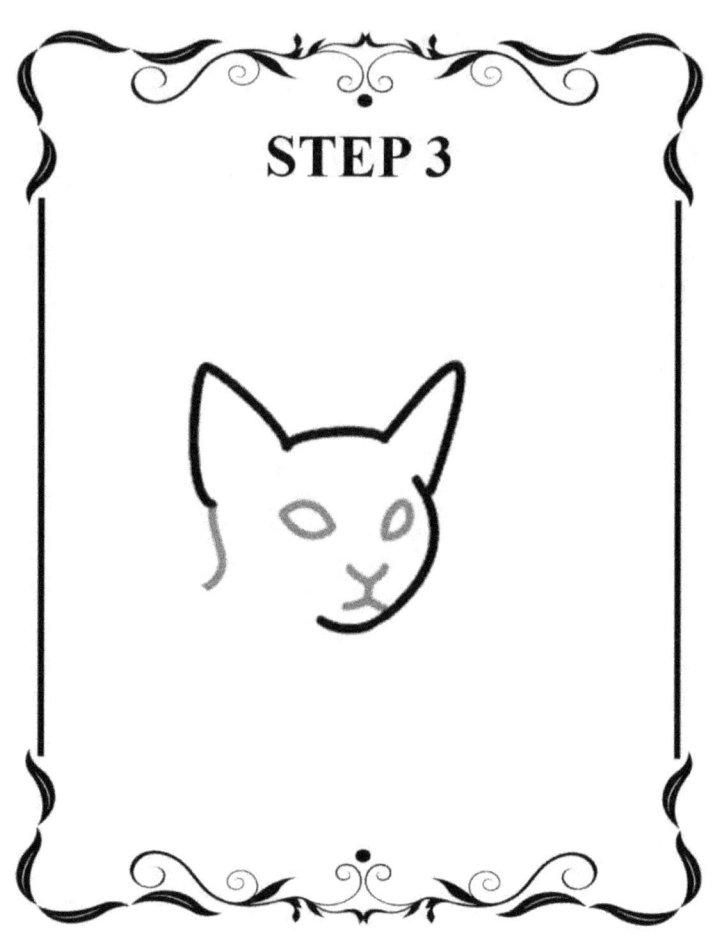

STEP 4

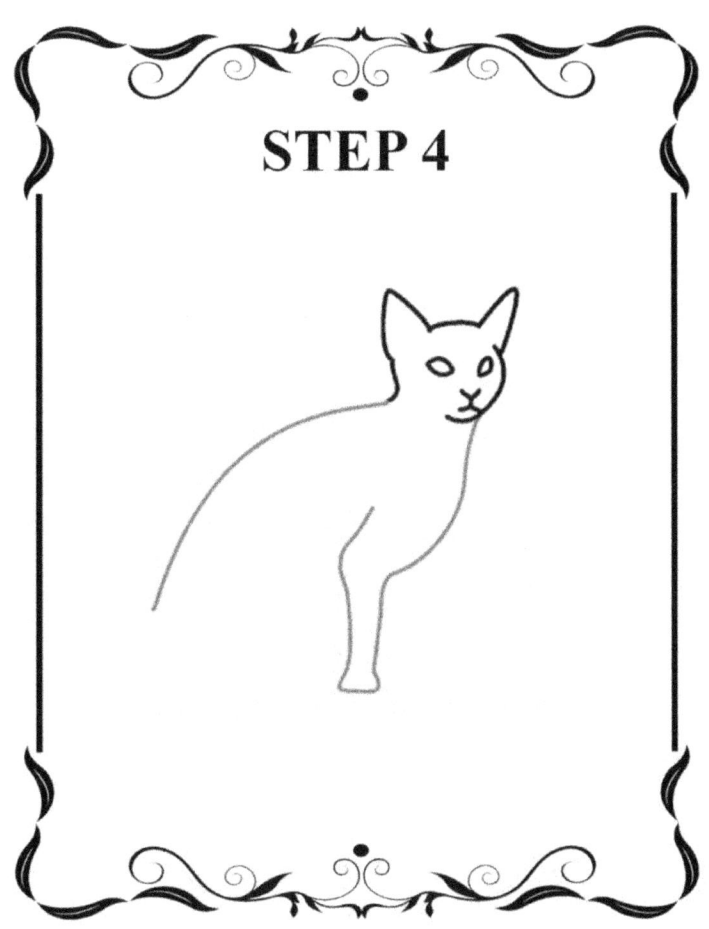

STEP 5

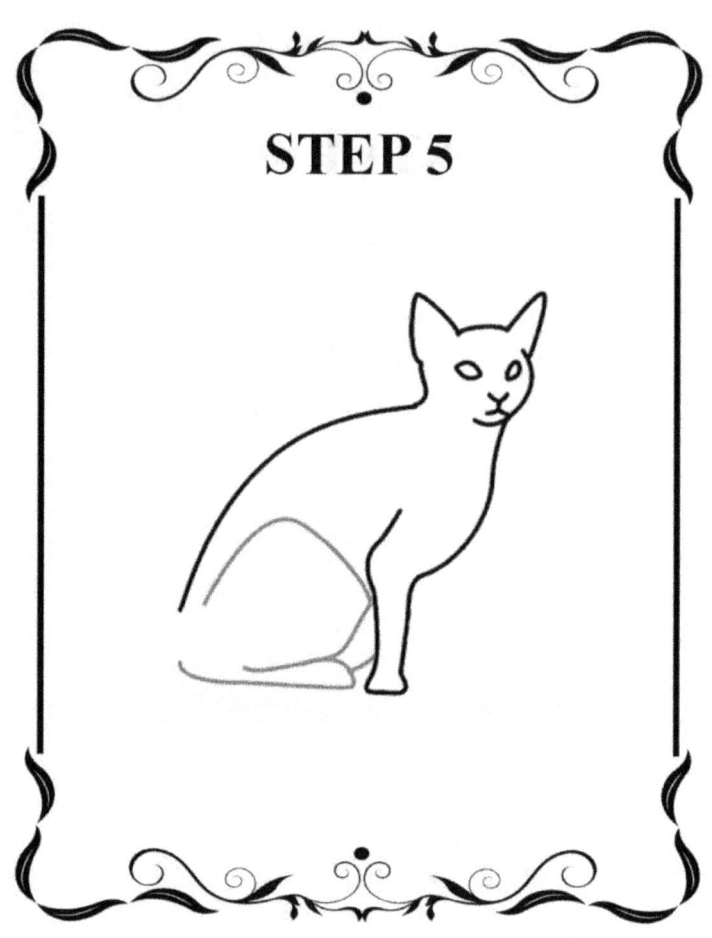

STEP 6

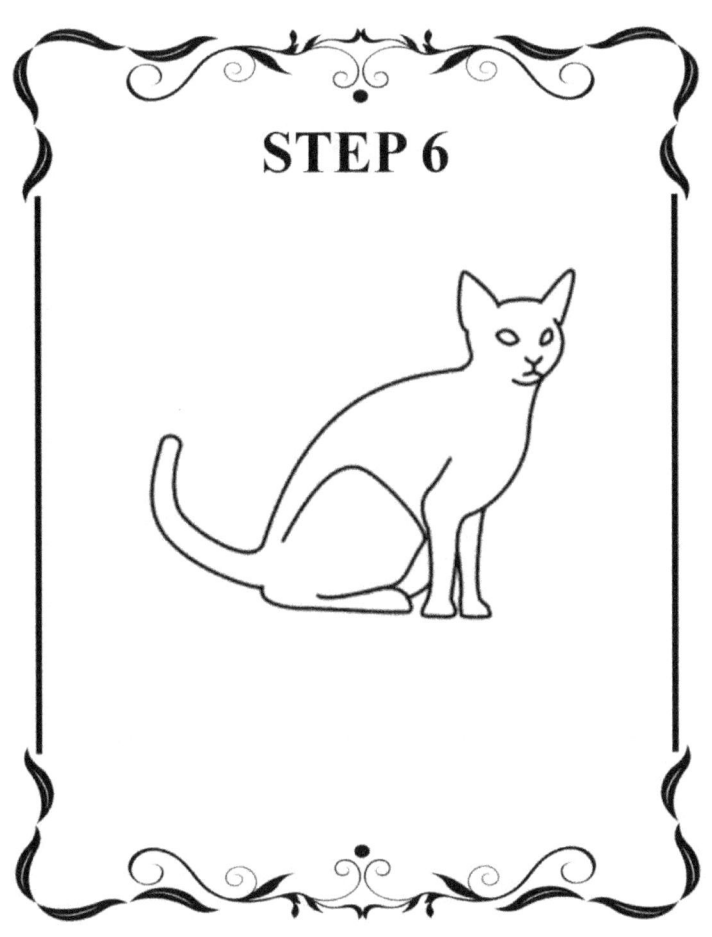

SKETCH
CAT

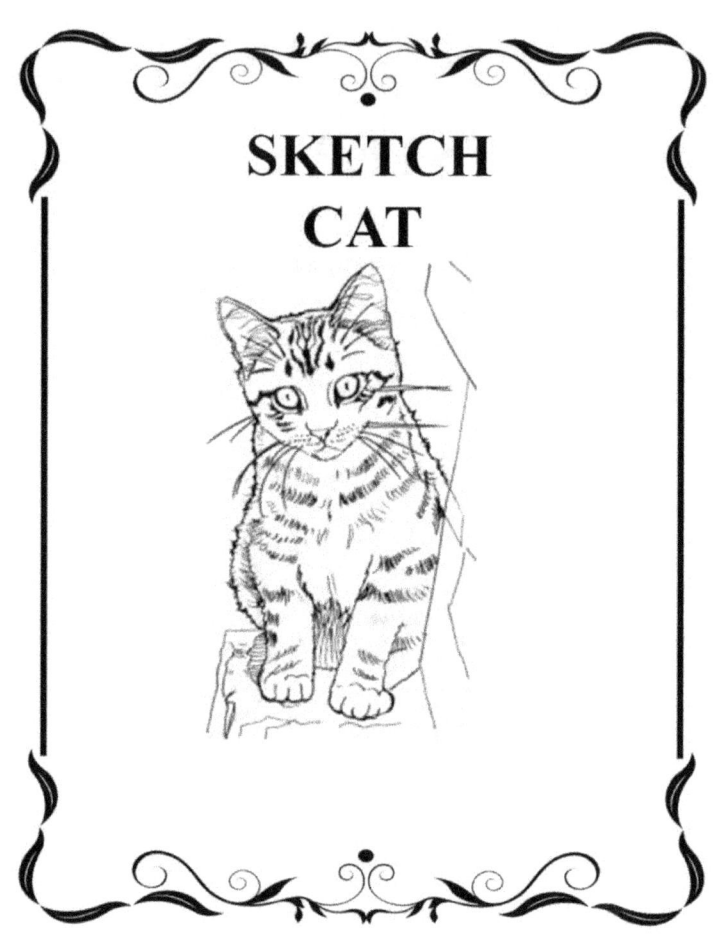

STEP 1

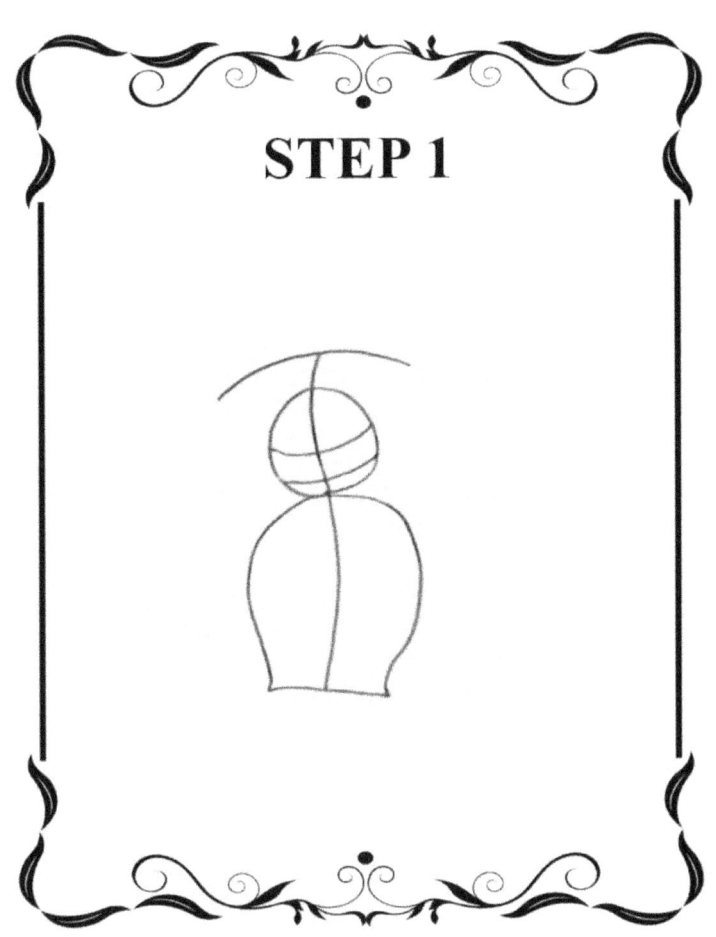

STEP 2

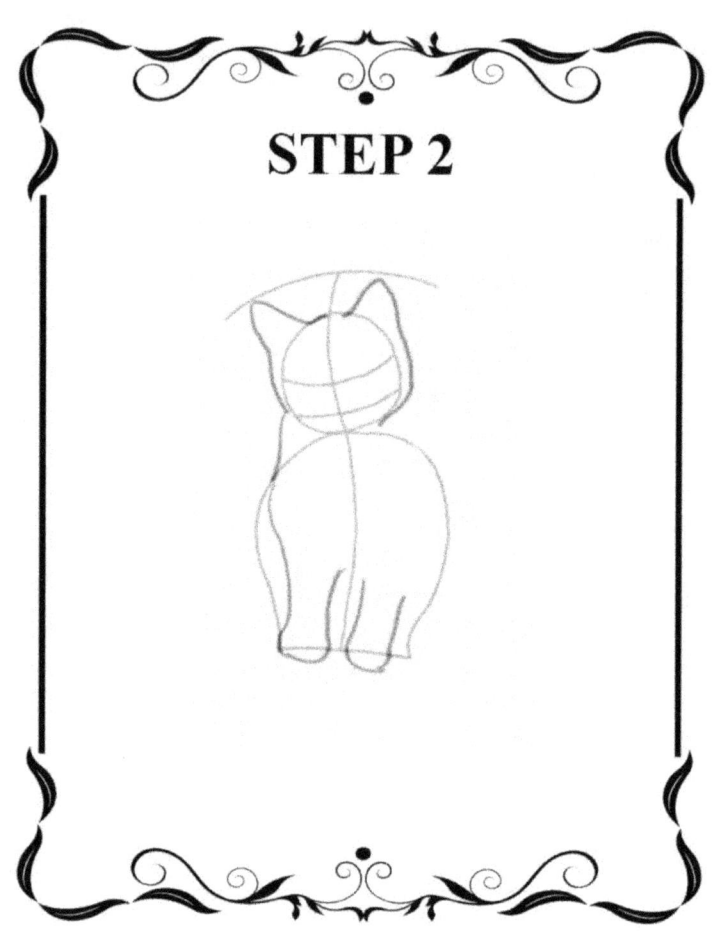

STEP 3

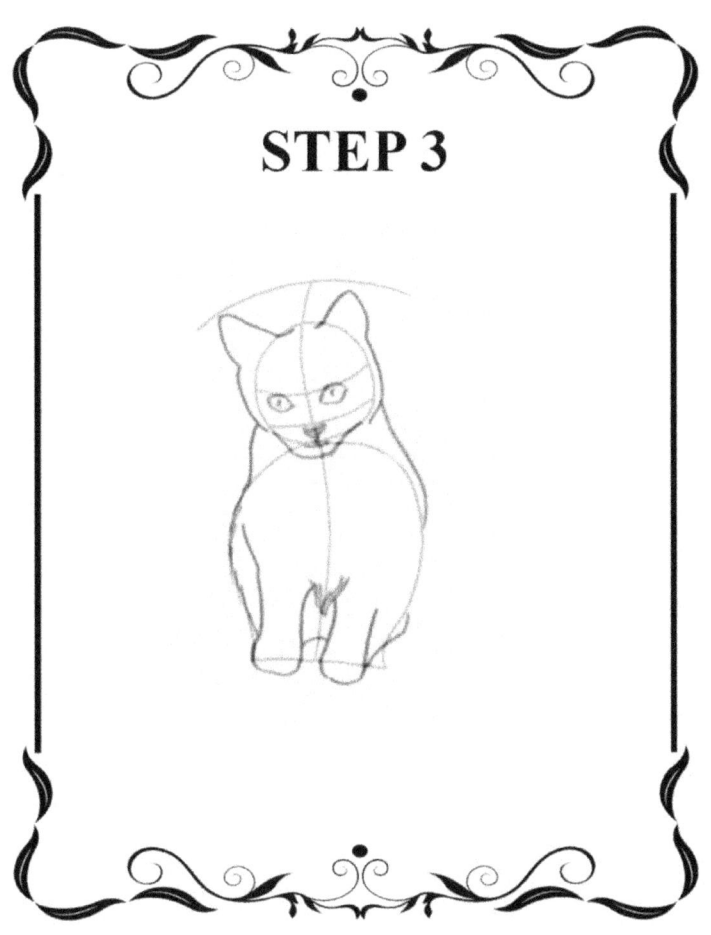

STEP 4

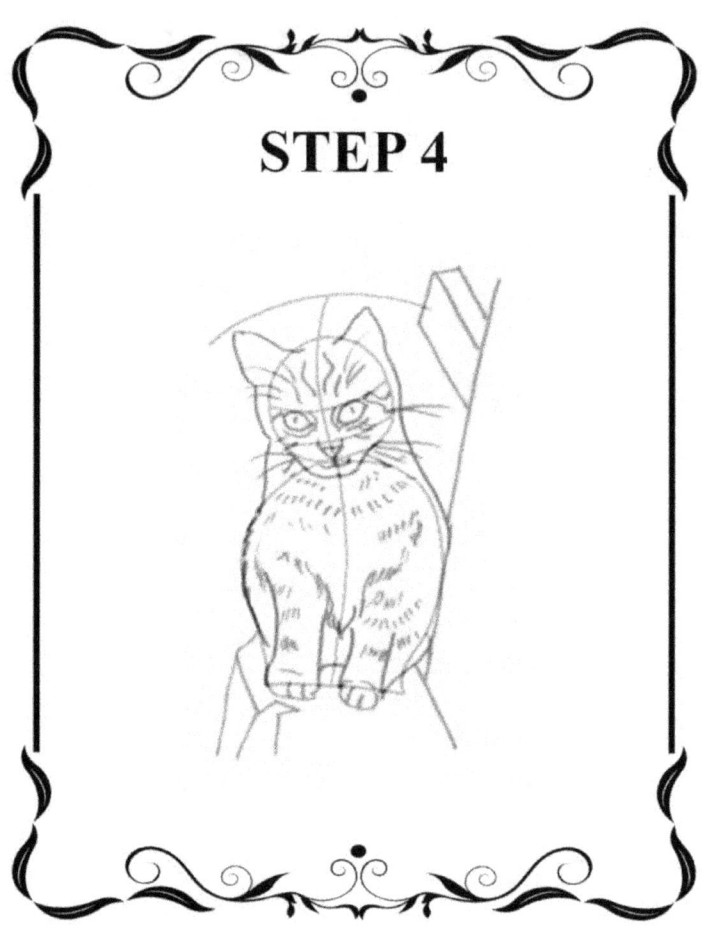

STEP 5

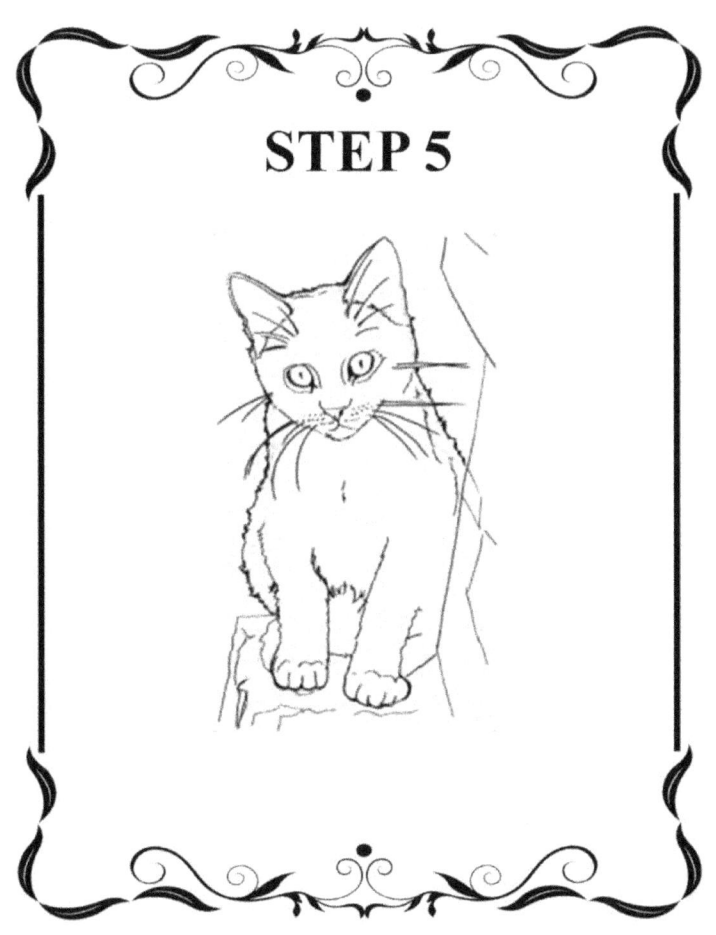

STEP 6

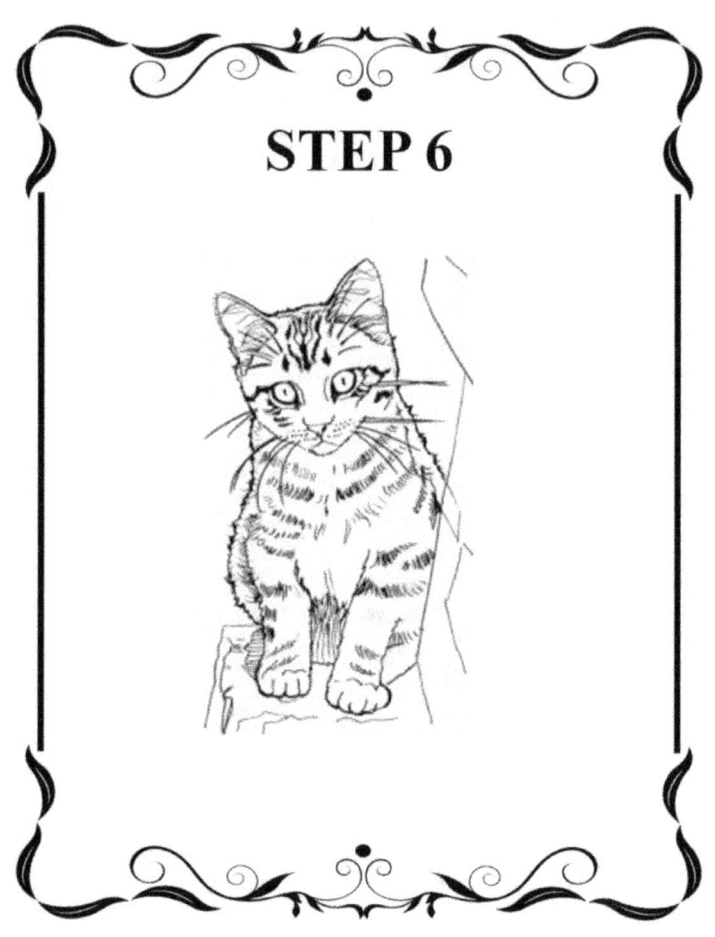

STANDING CAT

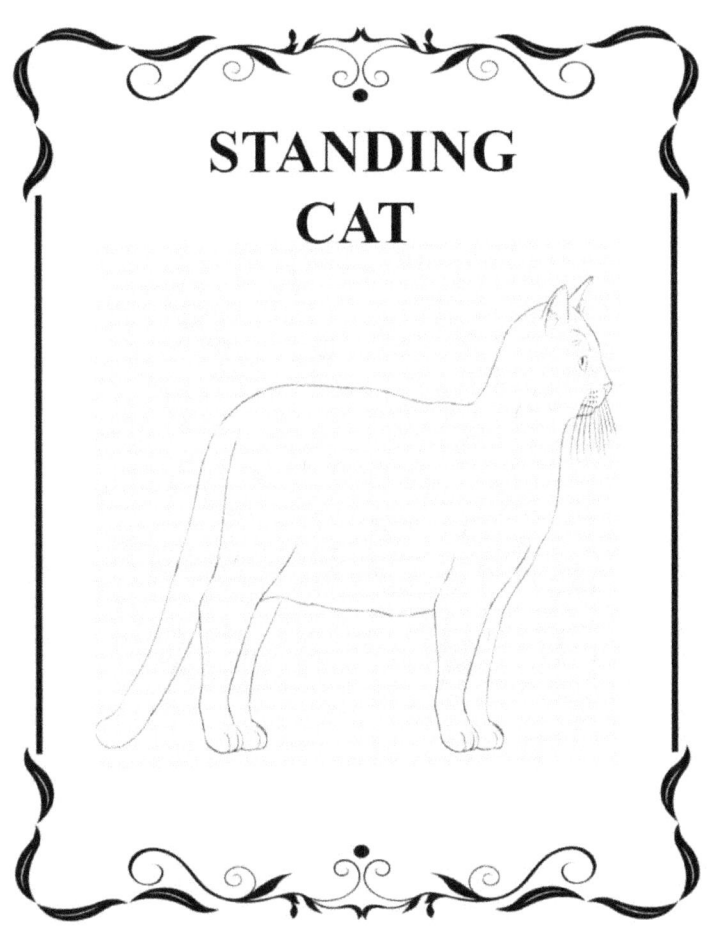

STEP 1

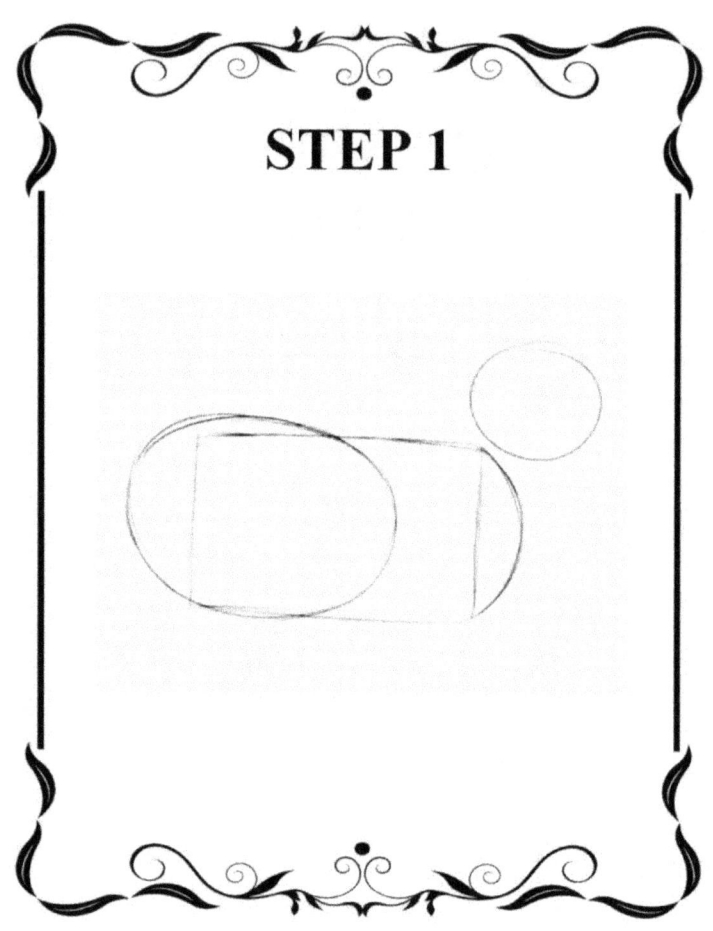

STEP 2

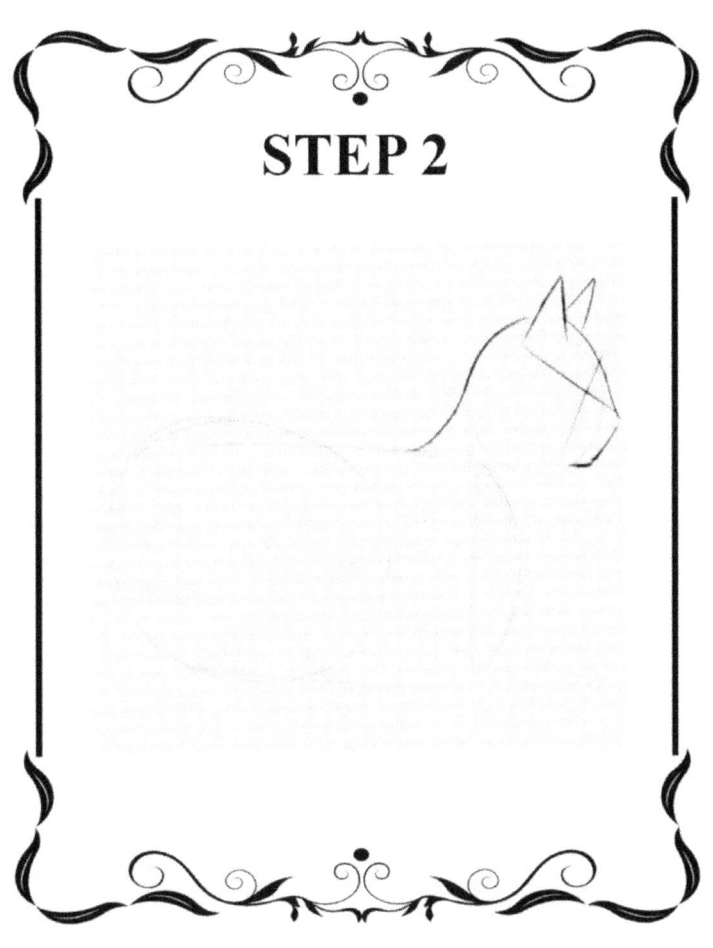

STEP 3

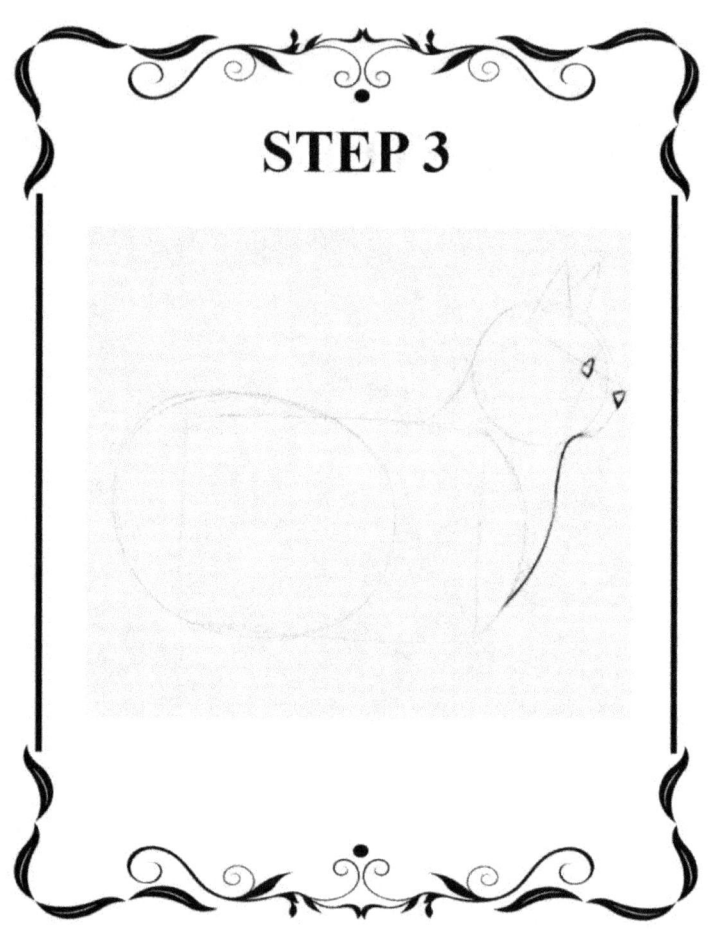

STEP 4

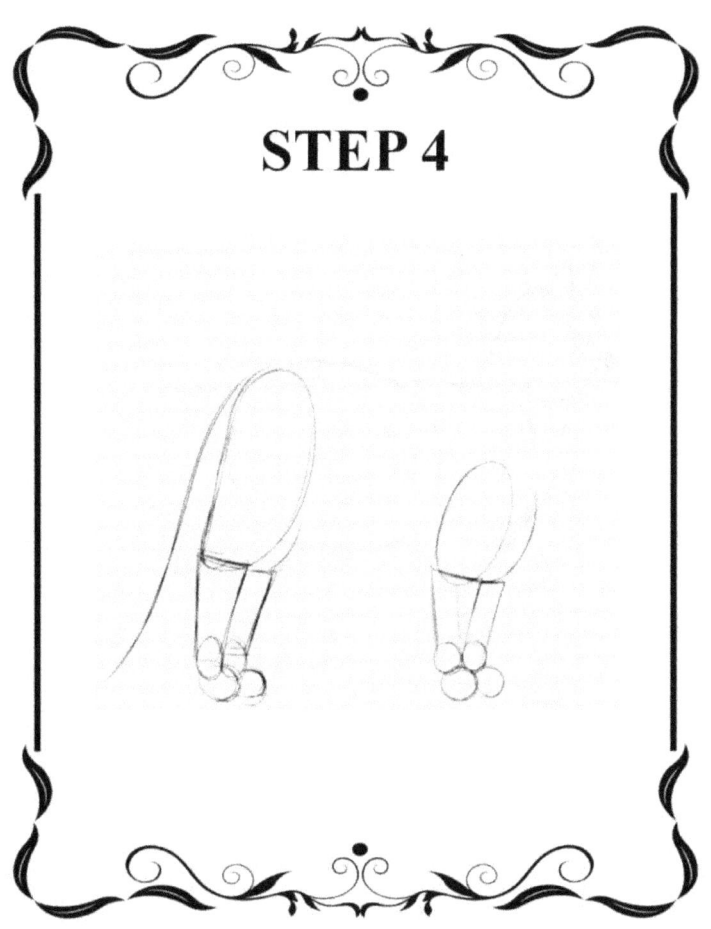

STEP 5

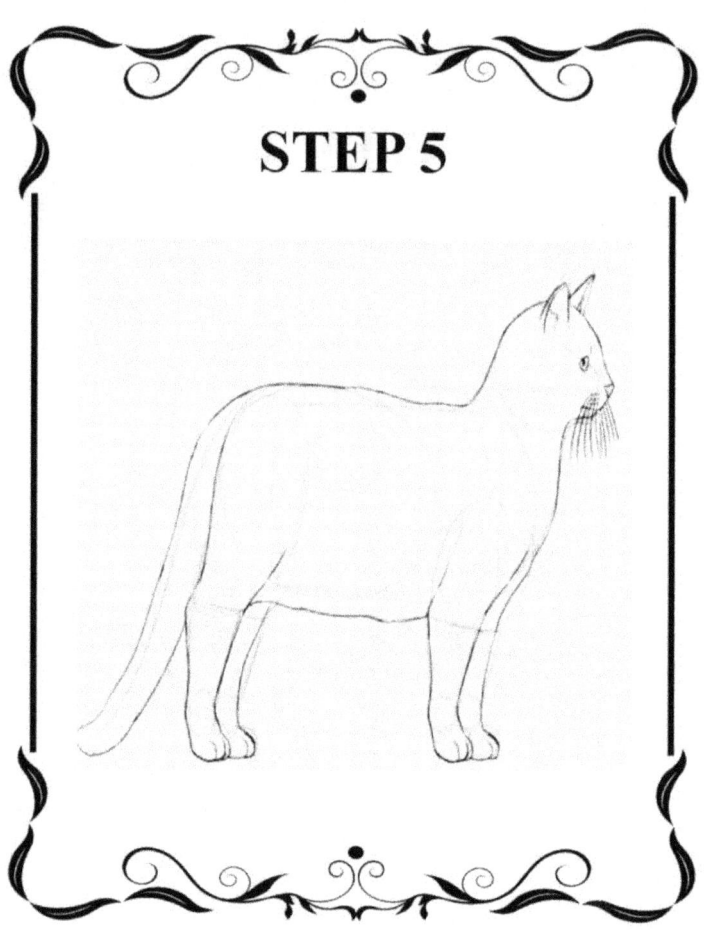

STEP 6

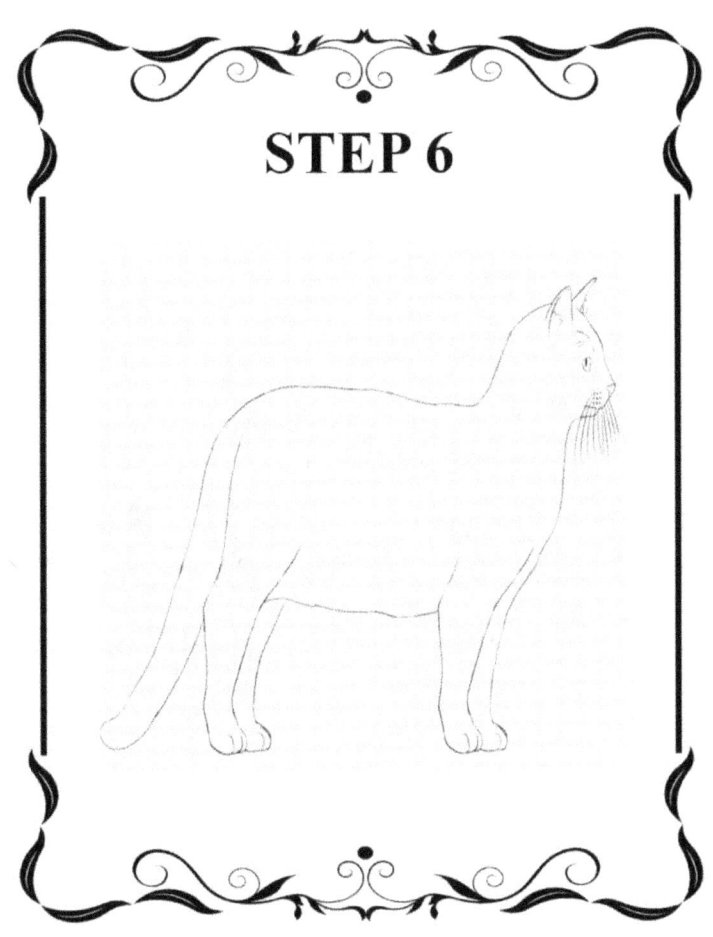

WILD CAT

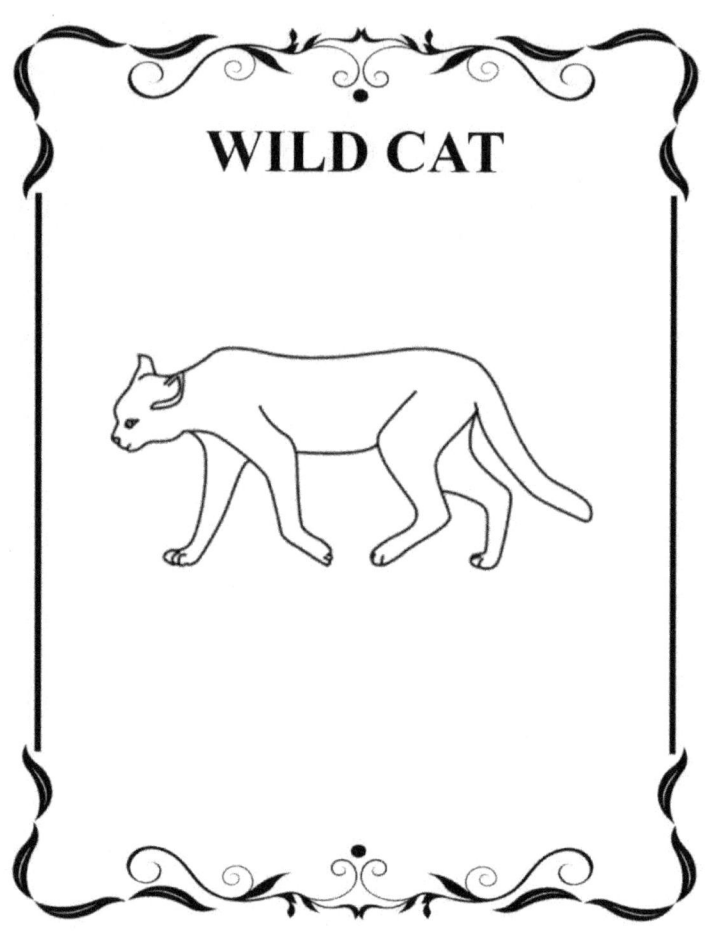

STEP 1

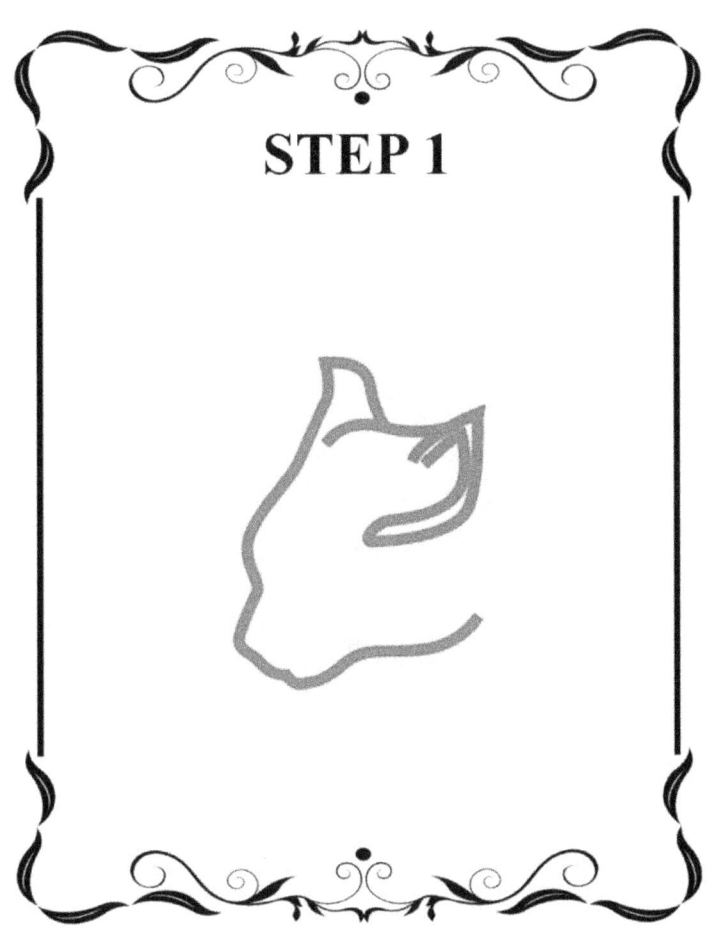

STEP 2

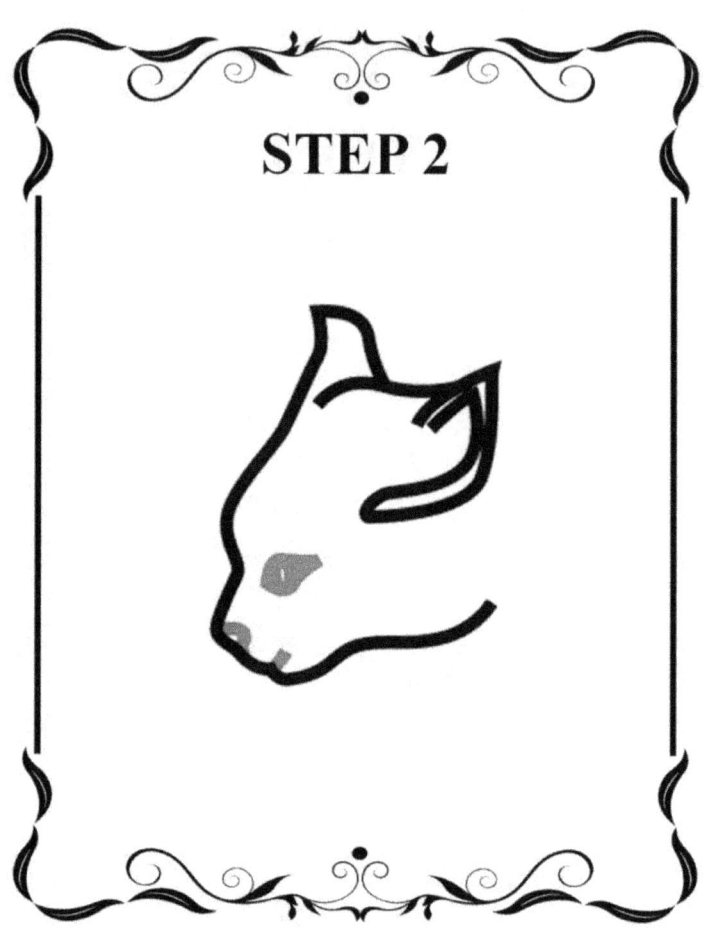

STEP 3

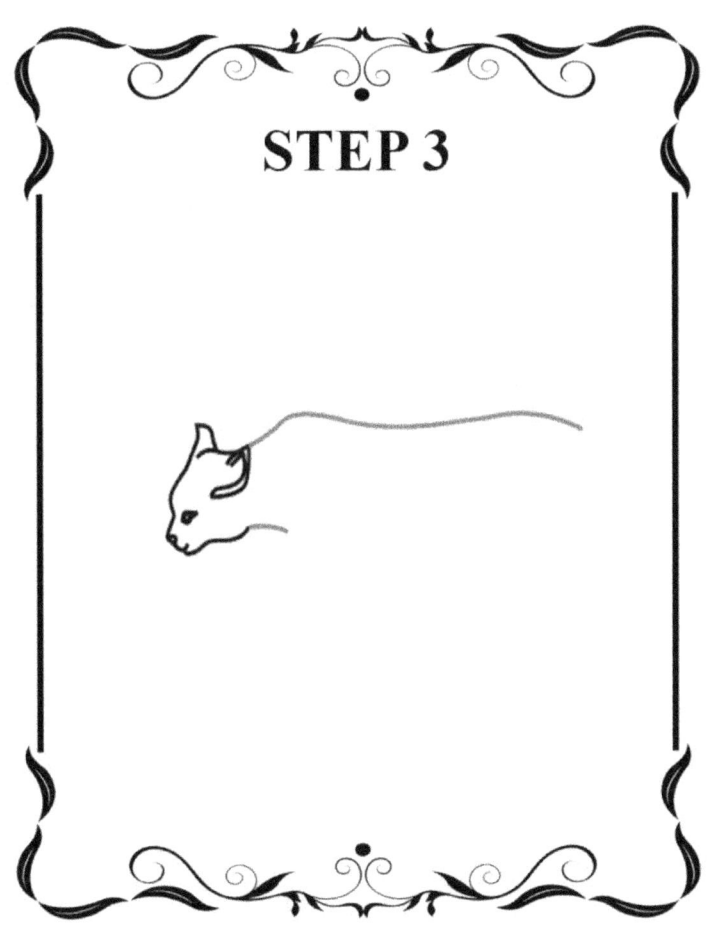

STEP 4

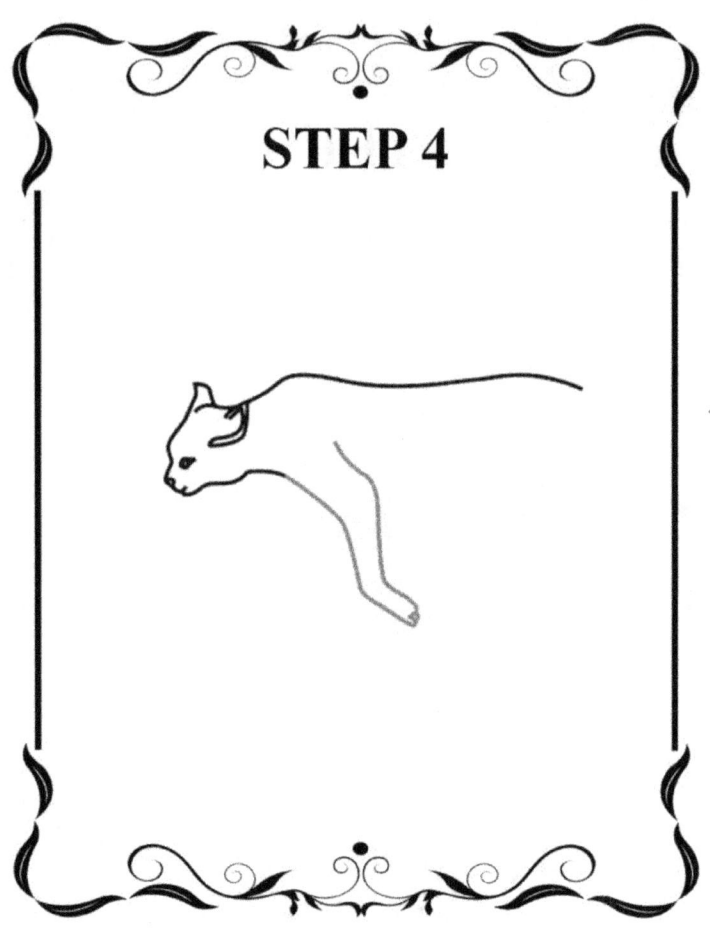

STEP 5

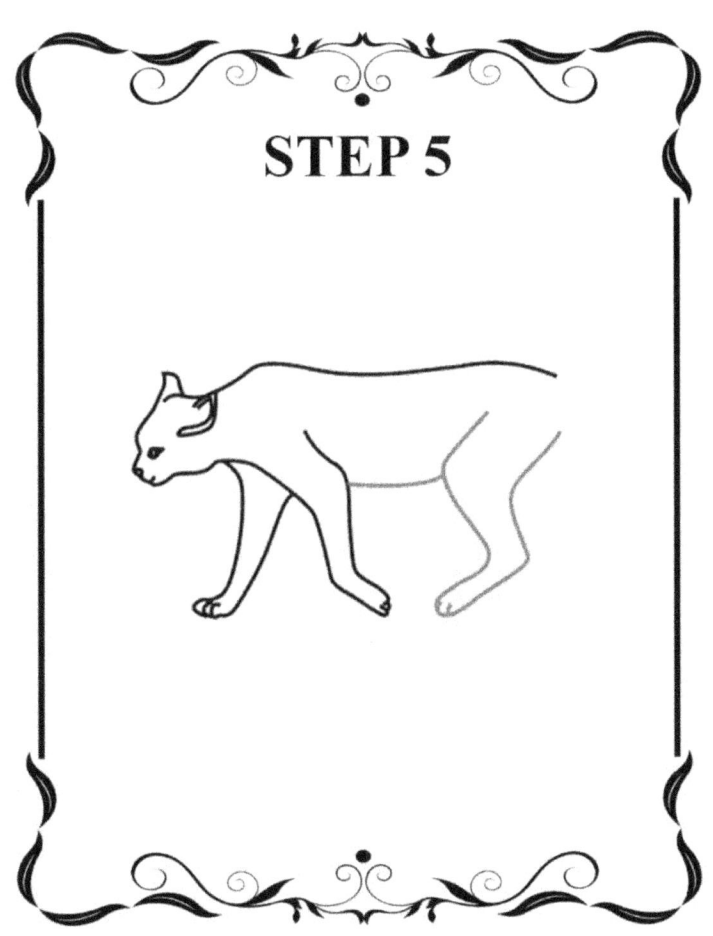

STEP 6

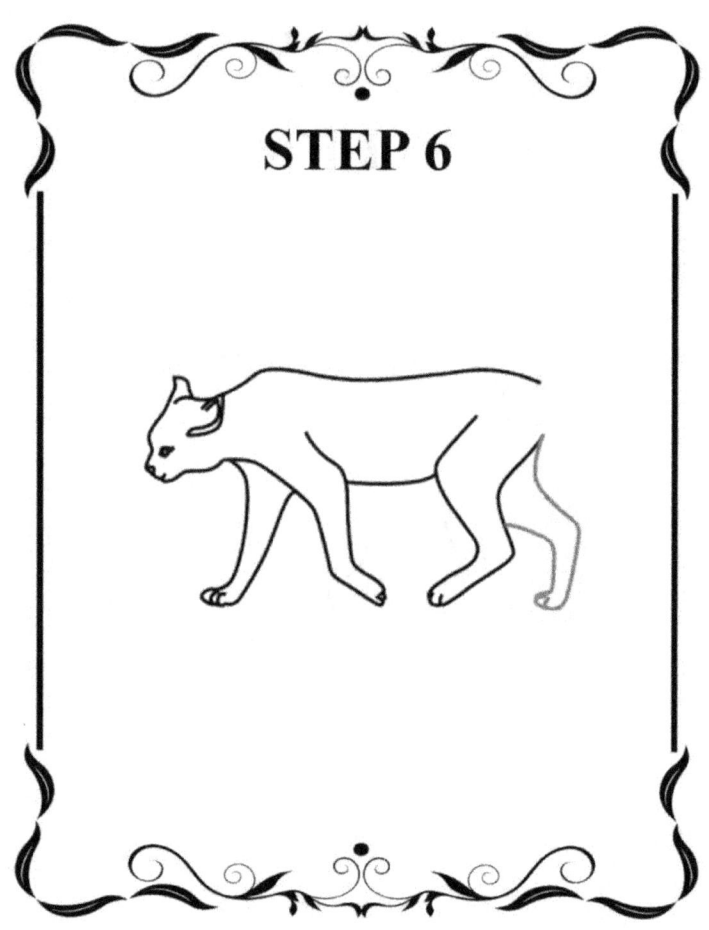

STEP 7

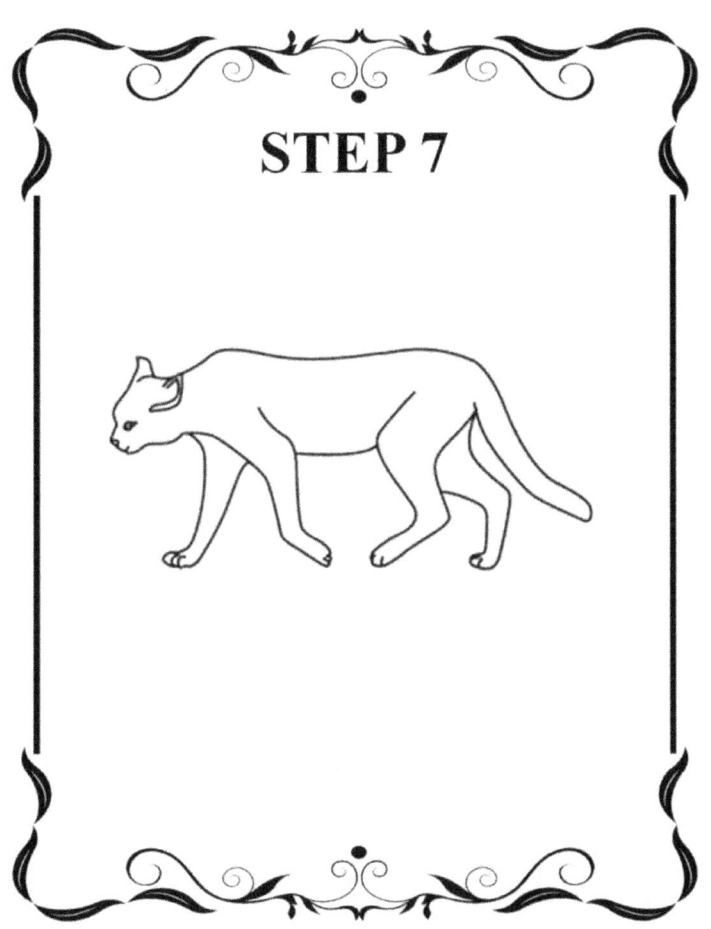

www.ingramcontent.com/pod-product-compliance
Lightning Source LLC
Chambersburg PA
CBHW071630170526
45166CB00003B/1267